ANSWERS ABOUT THE AFTERLIFE

ANSWERS ABOUT THE AFTERLIFE

A Private Investigator's 15-Year Research
Unlocks the Mysteries of Life after Death

Bob Olson

Building Bridges Press

Published by Building Bridges Press.

Because of the ever-changing nature of the Internet, all Web addresses and links contained within this book might have changed since the publication of this book and might no longer be valid.

Library of Congress Cataloging-in-Publication Data

Olson, Bob.

    Answers about the Afterlife: A Private Investigator's 15-Year Research Unlocks the Mysteries of Life after Death / Bob Olson

    p. cm.

    ISBN 0-9656019-8-6

    1. Self-Help—Death & Grief. 2. Spirituality—New Age. 3. Near-Death Experiences. 3. Past Lives. I. Title.

First Printing: April 2014

ISBN 0-9656019-8-6

Printed in the USA

Cover design by Peter O'Connor at BespokeBookCovers.com

ISBN-13: 9780965601986

ISBN: 0965601986

Library of Congress Control Number: 2014902714

Building Bridges Press, Kennebunkport, ME

Building Bridges Press

Also by Bob Olson

Afterlife TV with Bob Olson
Interviews about life after death using an online video format.
http://www.AfterlifeTV.com

Best Psychic Directory
A directory of 800 psychics and mediums by location.
http://www.BestPsychicDirectory.com

Best Psychic Mediums
Bob's "tested" list of psychics, mediums & more.
http://www.BestPsychicMediums.com

Psychic Medium Workshop
A home-study workshop for psychics & mediums.
http://www.PsychicMediumWorkshop.com

Dedication

To my father whose passing became the catalyst for my investigation
of life after death. Since his physical death, my father has assisted my
research and writing from his home in the spiritual dimension and
has attended every one of my readings with mediums. His example
has taught me that our human experience does not end upon our
physical death; but rather, it continues with our ongoing interactions
with loved ones on the physical plane.

Bob Olson, Sr. 1932 – 1997

Acknowledgments

This book would not exist without the infinite love, patience, and support of my radiant wife, Melissa, who for some reason has allowed me to be her best friend since she was 12 and I was 15 years old. When she was 11 and we were first getting to know one another, she purchased a book for me as a gift titled *Don't Be Afraid To Die* by Gladys M. Hunt. I'm not sure if she purchased it because of my fascination with death or because it cost only $1.25. Nonetheless, as odd as the book's subject might have seemed to me at that time, I loved it because it came from her. And I still have it today, 36 years later.

Melissa has read every word of this book about one million times during the 3-plus years that I wrote it. Her editing and suggestions on content and phraseology hold so much more importance than anyone will ever understand, and I am grateful beyond expression for her assistance.

I must also acknowledge my friends and family members who have supported my passion in this field for many years. The journey would not have been as enjoyable if not for your support. You've listened to me enthuse about my latest discovery, experience, reading, or interview with both love and grace. And if you were ever bored by my stories, it never showed.

And what would I know if not for the people who have assisted me with my investigation of life after death. So I acknowledge the practitioners who have given me experiences, the people who have allowed me to interview them about their experiences, and the experts who have taught me what they have learned from their own research. This includes my guests on AfterlifeTV.com, the authors of books I've read, and the mediums who have allowed me to test what is possible with their abilities.

I'm also sincerely grateful to my audience—those people who find benefit in my work. I appreciate your encouragement, enthusiasm, and support for my investigations, my articles, my websites, and my videos. You are my muse as it was your life, your grief, and your questions that filled my mind when I wrote this book. And if you are reading this, then it is also you who has purchased my book. There would be no book if not for you, so I thank you.

Finally, I must thank my spirit guides, including deceased loved ones who have guided me in one way or another. Let me first say that you must be some of the most patient spirits of the Universe. More than that, however, you have guided me to know a life that leaves me feeling blessed every day of my existence. I thank you for your guidance, and I thank you for being my friends. See you when I get home. Please leave the light on.

Contents

PART THREE
Questions about the Afterlife / Spirit World

PART FOUR
Questions about Spirits, Angels, and Ghosts

PART FIVE
Questions about the Wants and Needs of Spirits

PART SIX
Questions about Spirit Communication

PART SEVEN
Questions about Readings with Psychic Mediums

PART EIGHT
Questions about Suicide and Murder

PART NINE
Questions about Past Lives and Reincarnation

PART TEN
Questions about Near-Death Experiences

FINAL WORDS

How to Read This Book

When I first decided to write this book, I imagined that readers would be able to open the book up to any question and read the answer—that you could skip around and read these answers in any random fashion that you wish. While you are certainly welcome to take that approach, it wasn't long into the writing when I recognized that there's a chronology to these answers, meaning that early answers help you to understand later answers so that each answer builds upon the next.

Therefore, if you want to gain the most out of this book, my recommendation is that you read it from beginning to end. If you instead choose to skip around, you risk not fully understanding some of my later answers, especially the answers in the second half of this book, which get into more complex, and consequently more meaningful, insights about the afterlife.

You should also know to expect repetition in this book for three valuable reasons. One, I can only answer some questions fully by repeating something I've already written. Two, because some readers will skip around and only read the questions that interest them, I must repeat some information in order to give a complete answer. And three, I come from the mindset that "repetition is the mother of all learning" and that repetition helps us to learn and retain new information. So when you notice information that's being repeated in more than one answer, know that it's intentional to help you gain the most from this book.

INTRODUCTION

—⚏—

THE FOUNDATION OF THIS BOOK

There is one fact with which I must begin any introduction to a book, workshop, or lecture about the afterlife—it is that we do not know all the answers. Having said that, we do have a great deal of evidence about spirits, spirit communication, and the spirit world from which we can draw persuasive conclusions. And for the most part, these conclusions are true. However, they are not accurate.

"True but not accurate" simply means that these conclusions are true as far as our human minds can comprehend them, but they are not entirely accurate from the viewpoint of the spiritual realm. Nonetheless, our brains are of the physical world, so this is apt to be the most complete understanding we're capable of having. As times change and the veil between the physical and spiritual thins, it's possible that we'll gain a deeper understanding of life after death. But living in our current reality, "true but not accurate" still holds the power to an awareness that allows us to understand the really big questions about life, death, and spirituality. And that's what this book is about.

So what evidence do we have? In brief, we have the accounts of people with near-death experiences, folks who certainly have a much better idea than most of us about what it's like on the other side of our physical existence (the spiritual realm). We also have what people in spirit have communicated through mediums and channelers. Plus there are the accounts of individuals who have had spiritual regressions (often called "life-between-lives" regressions) and have traveled into the spirit world while under hypnotic trance. We even have people who have had shared-death experiences, where they shared the experience of their dying loved ones being welcomed home by their friends and family in spirit.

Of course, I'm just scratching the surface here regarding the vast array of evidence that exists to teach us about life after death, which I'll cover below and throughout this book. But it's important you understand this book is not about documenting all the evidence and explaining it; rather, this book is about answering the most common questions people have about the afterlife—based on that evidence.

There's simply not enough room in one book to both provide these answers *and* provide a detailed analysis of all the evidence. Since plenty of books already hash over all the evidence from either a scientific or metaphysical standpoint, this book is here to deliver the answers that are based on that evidence from a practical investigator's assessment. Consequently, as I give you my answers in this book, I'll also provide plenty of resources where you can read more about the evidence and the detailed analysis of it.

It's important that I explain how I arrived at these answers. I'm an investigator, not a psychic, medium, or channeler. I'm also not a scientist. I'm an investigator who draws conclusions based on an examination of the evidence using logic, reason, and pragmatism. I begin my investigations without bias or expectation and draw conclusions only *after* gathering and examining the available evidence. In other words, I look at the evidence first and draw my conclusions second.

Science, to an investigator, is merely one means of gathering evidence, not an intended means of proving anything by itself. In a criminal court of law, for instance, scientific evidence is just one of many pieces of evidence considered in determining an alleged criminal innocent or guilty. Judges and juries also consider physical evidence, witness accounts, motives, and past criminal histories, to name just a few. So this is also true when investigating the afterlife—scientific evidence is merely one source of many.

For example, double-blind studies of psychic mediums provide valuable evidence that mediums have exceptional abilities for knowing facts that they couldn't know if not for an intuitive ability. But no scientist has "proven" that mediums actually communicate with spirits. That would be a conclusion one would have to draw based on the evidence. And there's one main reason that someone has yet to "prove" that the afterlife exists: it's because proof is subjective—everyone must decide for himself.

The process of the investigator has been used in our civil and criminal court systems for as long as those institutions have existed. The legal system that holds our society together depends upon it. Logic, reason, and pragmatism, therefore, become part of the investigator's skill. In this way, judges and juries resemble investigators too because they all look at the evidence and base their conclusions using their own subjective reasoning. In fact, that's how most of us navigate our way through life. We are each investigators of our own life, making choices, interpretations, and decisions based on the evidence before us.

I began investigating the afterlife after the passing of my father in 1997. Because I was skeptical about life after death and had little spiritual foundation or understanding, I became curious about what happened to my father after his passing. So I decided to use my skills as a private investigator (my career at that time) to investigate the afterlife.

It wasn't until January 1999, however, that I first gathered evidence of life after death during a reading with a psychic medium (what many are now just calling a medium). Because it took two years to find evidence, I often say that my investigation began in 1999. That is certainly when it kicked into high gear, and I began to investigate life after death as a full-time passion. And it hasn't stopped yet.

Because I've had the luxury of investigating the afterlife on a full-time scale for all these years, the answers in this book are as realistically accurate as anyone can offer. And because I'm connected with so many gifted practitioners, credible experts, and celebrated authors in this field, I also know what others have been teaching. So I'll share with you what the most common beliefs are on particular subjects even if they happen to be in conflict with my own conclusions.

Because I sometimes disagree with what other people are teaching about the afterlife, I feel it's important that you see all sides to every answer so that you can decide which answer resonates most with your own experiences and beliefs. After all, it's not what I've concluded or what someone else believes that matters in the end; it's what you choose to believe that's most important.

The biggest problem I see occurring in this field is that people tend to pass along information about the afterlife without necessarily thinking it through. They simply accept it as true because someone else taught it to them, probably someone who learned it from someone else who, again, learned it from someone else. What they often don't realize, however, is that some of these answers were invented based on outdated and erroneous beliefs (and data) that no longer make any sense. Yet few people question these outdated answers, so they keep getting passed along.

For instance, a *few* psychic mediums teach about the afterlife based on what they learned from other mediums—not based on the evidence before them (their own spirit communication). Once they learned a false answer from somebody else, it led them to misinterpret the evidence before them because they already had expectations; that is, they made the evidence "fit" what they already believed rather than looking at the evidence first and drawing their conclusions second (as an investigator would do).

Some of the answers in this book may very well shake things up in this field. That's good. I want people to take a second look at the evidence before them and, likewise, take a second look at what they believe. Rather than continue to pass down the same outdated answers, it's time that we all start questioning those answers and rethink them for ourselves.

Consequently, you can read this book confidently knowing that this is not another rehashing of all the same answers presented by others for hundreds of years. Therefore, if I've included answers in this book that are in agreement with what you've already heard or read, you can be certain that they too have been squeezed through the ringer of practical analysis based on the latest evidence available.

Knowing all this, I hope you will use this book to inspire your own investigation into the afterlife rather than take my answers as the final word. Let my answers in this book help you to see the bigger picture, which might include two or three opposing beliefs, so that you can draw your own conclusions. Since proof is subjective, all that really matters is that you determine what equals proof to you. Even if it is different than what I believe or others believe, it's what feels right and sacred to your life and spiritual growth that really matters.

Now here is my list of some of the more compelling evidence of the afterlife that I have investigated. It is this evidence that has served as the foundation for the answers in this book. I won't necessarily repeat all the evidence as I write my answers about the afterlife, so review this list every now and then to remind yourself of the evidence my conclusions are based upon.

1. PSYCHIC MEDIUMS: There are numerous types of psychic mediums with particular specializations, including evidential mediums (who communicate with spirits, giving people names, dates, and detailed descriptions of what they looked like, how they died, and what their personality characteristics were before passing), spirit artists (who draw the spirits they can see), psychic medium detectives (who help police solve crimes with the assistance of people in spirit), missing persons psychic mediums (who help find missing people), historical psychic mediums (who provide insight into historical places or objects), medical intuitives (who help doctors diagnose physical ailments), and animal communicators (who communicate with dogs, cats, horses, birds, and reptiles, including those that have died).

Psychic mediums offer some of the most compelling evidence of life after death. And they do this in private sittings and from stages in front of small and large audiences of 30 to 3,000 people.

2. PAST-LIFE REGRESSIONS: When hypnotic regressionists use guided meditation techniques to lead ordinary folks into a semiconscious memory of a past life, it's called a past-life regression. After guiding the sitter into the past-life memory, the regressionist then asks questions about what the sitter is wearing, seeing, smelling, tasting, and hearing in the past life. The sitter will often know their name (first name, at least) in that lifetime, the year, details about their personality and appearance, information about their friends and family members, and most often, details about some significant event in their life as well as how they died.

A popular book on this subject is *Many Lives, Many Masters* by Dr. Brian Weiss. Dr. Weiss, a graduate of Columbia University and Yale Medical School, was a bit skeptical when his psychotherapy patient, Catherine, began recounting the details of her past-life traumas. These past-life reviews, however, set Catherine free from the anxiety and nightmares that led her to seek Dr. Weiss's treatment in the first place. Dr. Weiss was then captivated by the idea of using past-life regression as a treatment tool, and the world became hypnotized by his best-selling books that retold the particulars of his patients' healing journeys in remarkable detail.

So the afterlife question provoked by past-life regression is this: if we live multiple lifetimes, is this evidence that we don't really die and that there is a place or dimension between lives?

3. NEAR-DEATH EXPERIENCES AND OUT-OF-BODY EXPERIENCES: When people die for a brief time (a few seconds to a few minutes) and then come back to life, some have what is called a near-death experience (NDE), which is an experience where they leave their body, view their body from above, and then often go into a light they describe as the spirit world. Here, deceased loved ones or other spiritual beings (nonphysical beings) greet them before they are told they must go back to their physical life.

In many cases, information that the person obtained while out of their body has been confirmed—for instance, what doctors said or did in the emergency room—that the person lying dead could have otherwise never known. Doctors have tested this phenomenon in many ways with remarkable results.

Some people don't travel to the spirit world, but they do leave their body, which is known as an out-of-body experience (OBE). People do not have to die to have this experience. Those who have become proficient in having intentional OBEs claim to travel to other lands and other dimensions, including the afterlife. For books on intentional OBEs, check out *Adventures Beyond the Body* by William Buhlman and *Navigating the Out-of-Body Experience* by Graham Nicholls.

Two near-death experience researchers who have made major impacts on what we know in this field are Dr. Raymond Moody (see his book *Life after Life: The Investigation of a Phenomenon—Survival of Death*) and P. M. H. Atwater (see her book *Near-Death Experiences: The Rest of the Story*).

4. PAST-LIFE RECALL: Art Linkletter used to say that "kids say the darndest things." Well, recent claims have been made that some kids talk about their former lifetimes. These children know their past-life names, what they did for a living, their friends' names, and even how they died in a past life. This phenomenon is called past-life recall.

A best-selling book titled *Soul Survivor*, by Bruce and Andrea Leininger, documented a boy's memory as a World War II pilot. The story is significant because the boy's parents eventually researched their son's claims (despite their skepticism). What they learned is that the man their son claimed to be actually existed 60 years prior, and many details given by their son were eerily accurate. As it turns out, there really was a World War II fighter pilot named James Huston who was killed in the Battle of Iwo Jima.

5. DEATHBED VISIONS (a.k.a. pre-death visions): Many dying people have claimed to see spirits—often deceased loved ones—welcoming them to the other side. These apparitions are there to prepare

them for their journey home and then escort them to the spirit world upon their death, say experts. While most of the evidence we have for this common occurrence consists of eyewitness accounts from surviving relatives or friends who were present when it happened, these incidents are so widespread, and with such interesting responses from the dying, many people believe they are real.

6. SHARED-DEATH EXPERIENCES: There are many claims of family members and friends who have shared their dying loved one's deathbed visions, called shared-deathbed experiences (or shared-death experiences). In these instances, people say that they too had an otherworldly experience that was similar to or exactly the same as their dying loved one's transition back to the spiritual world. Many believe it occurs because they're in the same room with the dying person, but not everyone who has experienced this phenomenon has been in the same room. People who have had shared-death experiences have seen spirits of deceased people, caught a glimpse of the spirit world, and even felt an alternate dimension, as if the dying person held open the door to eternity so they could experience what it is like for a moment.

7. DREAM VISITATIONS: It's natural that the bereaved long for contact from their deceased loved ones on the other side. Survivors want to know that their loved ones who have passed are okay, that they still exist in some form or another, and that they are watching over them from above. Well, some people claim to get this direct contact in their dreams. However, these aren't like most dreams, which are faintly recalled and often disjointed. Dream visitations from the dead are usually extraordinarily vivid and realistic, are filled with heartfelt emotion, and are remembered by the dreamer many years later in such lucid detail it's as if they had the dream the prior evening.

8. HAUNTINGS: Americans seem obsessed with ghosts and hauntings, yet what does a haunting prove? For me, hauntings are merely one piece of evidence of an afterlife. If ghosts exist, that would be evidence of the survival of consciousness.

There are two different classifications of hauntings: ghosts and energy imprints.

First, there are ghosts often referred to as earthbound spirits, which some believe are people who have died but have not gone into the light for various reasons. Others, myself included, believe ghosts are not earthbound but are merely loved ones in spirit trying to say hello, which happens to scare some people.

Second, there are energy imprints of traumatic events of the past. These are a different phenomenon altogether. Energy imprints are believed to be places where the energy of an event continues to exist, sort of like a holographic photograph. People who are sensitive to this energy can sometimes tap into it and recognize these imprints, which they often interpret as seeing or hearing a ghost. There really is no ghost, however, just the imprinted memory of some historical event that took place. These people are psychically tuning into an energetic memory.

9. NON-MEDIUM SPIRIT VISIONS: Mediums who see spirits are one thing, but what about the thousands of ordinary people who are not mediums but have experienced a vision of a spirit? Many people see visions of spirits at the foot of their bed or walking down their hallway. One woman I know saw her deceased husband walking up her stairway. Visions of spirits—usually deceased loved ones—are common, though it usually happens to most people only once. And then there are a few who see them regularly and even continue their relationship with the person in spirit over many years (see the book *The Afterlife of Billy Fingers* by Annie Kagan).

10. CHANNELING: As mentioned, mediums are people who claim to communicate with our deceased loved ones, so what are channelers? Channelers, also known as channels, claim to communicate with higher-level spirits, often group entities, for the purpose of conveying wisdom (as opposed to communicating messages from the dead to their surviving loved ones as mediums do). The most well-known channel of the past is Jane Roberts, who channeled a spiritual being named Seth (check out her book *Seth Speaks*), but there are many more who do this work today. One channel named Paul Selig has channeled three books: *I Am the Word*, *The Book of Love and Creation*, and *The Book of Knowing and Worth*. I recommend all three.

11. REINCARNATED PEOPLE: There are people who claim to be reincarnated versions of famous people of the past. Physically, their appearances are strikingly similar. They even share the same personality characteristics, skills, or talents—often long before they realize the similarities they have with the famous person. But are they really the same souls reincarnated into a different body in a different lifetime? Only a look at all the evidence, comparing the people who make these claims with the historical evidence of who they claim to be, can help us make a determination. I'm still unconvinced, but I find the subject fascinating.

12. ANGEL INTERVENTIONS: Some people who have escaped a seemingly inescapable tragic accident or crime claim that an angel intervened. Is it possible that angels exist among us to keep us alive or unharmed at times? And if this is real, are these deceased loved ones in spirit watching over them, or are there angels who exist just for this purpose? Furthermore, why are some people saved while others are not? These are all questions I have explored while interviewing people who claim to have had angel interventions. In the end, while the abundant stories of this kind are intriguing, the evidence is mostly hearsay (people's verbal reports without hard evidence).

13. LIFE-BETWEEN-LIVES REGRESSIONS: What happens if we have a past-life regression but continue to follow our existence after our death in that lifetime? That's what hypnotic regressionist Michael Newton asked himself years ago. What he found was that we leave our bodies and go into the spirit world to prepare for our next physical life. He called it the "life between lives." And this extended regression experience, which usually takes four to five hours to complete, allows individuals to learn about their soul group, why certain people are in their life, and even their purpose for being alive today. Michael Newton's books on this subject include *Journey of Souls* and *Destiny of Souls*.

14. CHILDREN'S SPIRIT CONTACT: It's possible that some children's imaginary friends aren't imaginary at all. In fact, it's quite likely that some imaginary friends are actually people in spirit. Are

these kids perhaps communicating with relatives or other people on the other side? That's what some parents have concluded since their children know things about their dead relatives—people who died before the child was born—when there is no other way for them to know.

Many children actually see people in spirit because they haven't yet learned to be skeptical. And many believe that children have the ability to see spirits because they have only been away from the spirit world a brief time. What's different about these incidents—as opposed to adult spirit visions, for instance—is the innocence and authenticity that children bring to these subjects.

15. PRE-BIRTH PLANNING: I believe that we plan our life experiences—at least our major challenges and relationships—before we are born. And there's convincing evidence to support this idea, most gained from working with mediums, channels, and regressionists. This subject is ripe with riveting stories that help people find meaning in their suffering in ways that will deepen your understanding of why bad things happen to good people. I highly recommend you read two books on this subject by Robert Schwartz titled *Your Soul's Plan* and *Your Soul's Gift*.

16. CHILDREN'S NEAR-DEATH EXPERIENCES: Near-death experiences of adults are interesting, but NDEs of children take it to a whole new level. Because of their authentic innocence, children's near-death stories are fascinating storytelling. And there are researchers who have dedicated their careers to researching this phenomenon.

17. PHOTOGRAPHS OF SPIRITS: There's a ton of photographs in existence that people claim captured the image of a spirit. In almost all cases, the photograph was taken of something else, and the spirit image was noticed later. Even when recognizing the opportunity for fraud in these cases, some of these photos are undeniably interesting and do serve as tangible evidence of life after death.

18. ELECTRONIC VOICE PHENOMENON: Many people have audio recordings that they claim have voices of spirits on them.

Normally, these are recordings of dead air taken by ghost hunters for this purpose. While fraud is easy to manipulate in these cases, it's a subject to consider and perhaps experiment with nonetheless. Again, when fraud can be ruled out, this too is tangible evidence of an afterlife.

19. SPIRIT COMMUNICATION THROUGH HYPNOSIS: People are realizing that they don't need a medium to communicate with their loved ones in spirit. Many are having direct contact with the deceased using hypnosis. This is where people use hypnosis to get into a relaxed state and then use visualization to connect with spirits. It's not nearly as common as mediumship but can be even more effective since the connection is more direct. In my first experience with this technique, I saw and felt the presence of my father in spirit. It was awe-inspiring.

20. ANIMAL COMMUNICATION: According to a 2011 survey by the Humane Society of the United States, 86 million people in the United States own cats and 78 million own dogs, with 62 percent of households owning a pet. Consequently, when pets die, many of these pet owners wonder if their animals went to the afterlife. To answer these questions, we have animal communicators who communicate with both living and passed pets and thousands of pet owners who believe their pets have sent them messages from the spirit world. I too have tested animal communicators successfully, leaving me with compelling evidence that these pet mediums made contact with my deceased pets, mostly because they told me things that my pet would know yet the animal communicator could never know.

21. AFTER-DEATH COMMUNICATIONS: The phrase 'after-death communication' (ADC) was coined by ADC researchers Bill Guggenheim and Judy Guggenheim, who define ADCs as spiritual experiences that occur when you are contacted *directly* and *spontaneously* by a deceased family member or friend *without* the use of psychics, mediums, rituals, or devices of any kind. The Guggenheims estimated that 50–100 million Americans—20 percent to 40 percent of the population of the

United States—have had one or more ADC experiences. Therefore, ADCs provide convincing evidence for life after death.

While some of the subjects listed above fall into this ADC category (deathbed visions, dream visitations, non-medium spirit visions), there are many more that could be added to this list (or at least be grouped with other ADCs). These include the following: sensing a presence, hearing a voice, feeling a touch, smelling a fragrance, electronic phenomena (e.g., a telephone call from a deceased loved one's cell phone that is off), miraculous coincidences, animal visitations (birds or butterflies, for instance), frequently finding coins or feathers.

People consider after-death communications to be signs from loved ones in spirit to communicate that they are okay, they are watching over them, and they are still a part of their lives. For more information on these phenomena, I highly recommend reading Bill Guggenheim and Judy Guggenheim's book, *Hello from Heaven*.

22. SPIRIT WRITING: Spirit writing, otherwise known as inspired writing, is when a person channels information, guidance, or answers from a spirit through typing or writing. In most cases, a person will ask a question and immediately begin typing the answer before their intellect can contemplate the question and provide the answer. Many non-mediums have used this approach to communicate with their loved ones, get advice, or channel wisdom. In fact, I have experimented with inspired writing myself with extraordinary success.

Similarly, automatic writing is where a person channels information from a spirit through typing or writing, but the automatic writer is able to carry on a separate conversation, read a book, or watch television while their fingers type the channeled information. Thus, automatic writing is a much more advanced form of inspired (or spirit) writing.

PART ONE

—m—

BIG-PICTURE ANSWERS THAT WILL IMPROVE YOUR COMPREHENSION OF THIS BOOK

What is the purpose of life from the soul's perspective?

Before I answer all the upcoming questions about death and life after death, I'd like to take a moment to discuss life. This one question and answer is going to give you a new perspective that should help you better understand all the upcoming answers in this book.

So many people ask about the meaning or purpose of life. While it took me years of investigation and experience in this field to understand it, the answer is that the meaning (or purpose) of life is to have experiences. It's really just that simple—life is about having experiences. And to take this one step further, life is about having experiences that our souls are unable to have in the spiritual realm.

As souls who exist eternally in the spirit world, which is always free from fear, suffering, and death, we choose a physical life as humans to know the experience of living in a domain where mortality is imminent.

When a being knows it can die, it changes everything. It creates fear and alters choices. When death is a potential occurrence, we think, say, and do things differently. We act out of survival. Even the possibility of injury, illness, or pain leads one to choose differently than if that person were immortal and invincible. And this is why living a human life is such an intriguing challenge for our souls. It's not an easy challenge. It's not even necessarily fun. It simply creates a new paradigm from which to have new experiences, experiences our souls are unable to duplicate in the spiritual realm.

I make this point early in this book for one important reason—so many folks believe that something has gone wrong in life when they meet challenges (disappointment, tragedy, suffering, loss, and pain), but life is about experiences, both positive and negative. Nobody promised us that we'd have only positive experiences. We learn just as much, if not more, from our challenging experiences as humans, and whether we want to accept it or not, this is what we signed up for as souls when we chose to have a physical life.

This doesn't mean that negative experiences are necessary or even unavoidable. There are many ways to increase our awareness, live in the present moment, and choose our responses to our experiences such that life leans toward the positive. But no one lives a life completely free of negativity, otherwise known as challenges that we might prefer to avoid.

If you can accept that life is about experiences rather than about being happy and easygoing all the time, then the answers in this book will digest easier. Yet even if you have some resistance to this idea, don't give up right away because you will better understand what this really means as you continue reading. And by the time you finish reading this book, you will not only comprehend this "life is about experiences" concept better, but you'll recognize why it will provide you with a greater sense of inner peace than the belief (and expectation) that life should only include happy and positive experiences.

—✕✕—

What is the difference between a soul and a spirit?

It would be difficult for you to understand some of the answers in this book without an initial understanding of my definitions for the words 'soul' and 'spirit.' Based on the evidence I've seen, this is how I perceive the relationship between soul and spirit. You don't have to fully understand or accept my definitions at this point, but it'll help you to understand my answers throughout this book.

The soul is our whole self, the eternal and spiritual aspect of who we are. Since I've seen evidence that we experience many human lives, the soul is what is experiencing all those lifetimes. So if my soul has had a lifetime as Bob, another lifetime as George, and another lifetime as Sarah, then Bob, George, and Sarah all come from the same soul.

I like to explain this using the analogy of the ocean and its waves. First, there is the ocean, then from that ocean come the waves. The ocean is the soul, and the waves are the spirits—in this case, the spirit of Bob, the spirit of George, and the spirit of Sarah. So Bob, George, and Sarah are like waves, and their soul is like the ocean.

Each spirit has its own individual characteristics, but each will also have some common characteristics of its soul. Because of this, another soul will always be able to recognize a spirit's soul identity because of those signature characteristics. In other words, my wife's soul will always be able to recognize my soul regardless of what life it is experiencing. Said another way, if we could watch videos of Bob, George, and Sarah, we would be able to recognize similarities among them, which would be these signature characteristics of their soul. We might recognize their soul in their eyes, their voice, or their mannerisms, but we'd recognize it for sure.

Now taking this a step further, when I die, my spirit as Bob will leave my physical body and return home to the spirit world. In essence, my spirit will rejoin my soul and remain as an eternal aspect of my soul. In the same way that my human personality as a teenager is always present within me as an adult, my spirit as Bob will always be present in my soul.

To keep the comparison going, Bob as a young boy, Bob as a teenager, Bob as a young adult, Bob as a middle-aged adult, and—if I live that long—Bob as an older adult are all different human aspects of my life as Bob, just as the spirit of Bob, the spirit of George, and the spirit of Sarah are all different aspects of my soul. You've probably heard people talk about their inner child. Well, there's also an inner teenager, inner young adult, and inner middle-aged adult as well. These are parts of me that never disappear even though I age and my appearance and personality change a little.

So the equivalent to any of these inner aspects of my self would be my soul's inner Bob, inner George, or inner Sarah. While the spirits of Bob, George, and Sarah returned to the spirit world, thereby rejoining my soul (their whole self), their individual essences always remain as part of that soul. Hence, they too do not disappear, meaning that I can always communicate with my father, who is in spirit, or my grandmother. It's not as if they disappear into their souls either. The truth is that they were never really separate from their souls in the first place, so saying that we "rejoin" our souls is more metaphorical than literal.

I don't want you to mistakenly think that the spirit and soul are ever separate as they are not. They feel to us as separate—as humans—but even now, we are connected to our souls. And when we leave our bodies and return to the afterlife, we don't technically reunite with our souls; it is more that we recognize our connection to our higher self, which we might not have recognized in the physical world.

When my soul chooses to experience a new life—let's say, as Julie— it will create a new spirit of itself. And that spirit will inhabit a physical human body that will be Julie. Therefore, when we discuss reincarnation later in this book, this question will help you understand that it's not really Bob who is reincarnating; it's Bob's soul, who is creating a new spirit (a new aspect of itself) that will be known as Julie.

Because Julie shares the same soul as Bob, George, and Sarah, if she ever experiences a past-life regression, she might have memories of one of those lifetimes. But to describe it more accurately, it's her soul's lifetimes that she's experiencing. Because she is the wave to her ocean (her soul), and they are therefore connected as one, she is able to recall the other lifetimes of her soul. The wave doesn't reincarnate as another wave. The ocean creates a new wave, which is connected both to the ocean and all the other waves that came before it.

Why is this important? Well, for example, many people worry that their loved one might reincarnate before they themselves die and return to the afterlife. This "soul versus spirit" explanation helps you understand that their loved one's spirit isn't actually who is reincarnating—it's their loved one's soul that has created a new spirit to experience another lifetime. So no matter how long a person lives, their loved one will always be there in the spirit world to greet them when they die.

—◇◇◇—

How do you define God?

If you understand the relationship between soul and spirit, as described above, then it's easy to understand my view of God. If you understand that one soul is made up of many spirits, then it's an easy transition to think of God as made up of many souls—all souls, to be specific.

So God is Source Energy (all that is), and all the souls that exist are extensions of Source. A spirit, on the other hand, is an extension of its soul. So we have Source, which experiences all that is through its souls, which experiences all that is through its spirits. So it's a pyramid that goes like this: God > Souls > Spirits.

In this way, each individual spirit (including you and me) is simply an extension of God. Even though we don't necessary feel it as humans, we are eternally connected to God at all times. Even more accurately, we are God; that is, we are God in the same way that your arms and legs are you. You are not all that God is, just as your left arm is not all that you are, but you are most definitely one with God.

For so many years, I struggled to understand God. Even as I began investigating the afterlife—which taught me so much more than I ever imagined it would—many of my questions about God and the afterlife eluded me, especially the big ones like why God allows suffering, why God allows children to starve, and why God allows war and terrorism.

It wasn't until I stopped thinking of God as a single entity—stopped imagining God as an emotional human being—that everything finally began to make sense. The more I investigated the afterlife, the more I heard testimony from spirits (through mediums), and the more I interviewed people who had near-death experiences, the more I could no longer envision God as a person and instead began to view God as Creative Intelligence, Source Energy, or Universal Energy—the one force that connects everyone and everything together.

Viewing God as the Universe eliminated the human qualities I was giving God, which were confusing me. When you think of God as creative intelligence, you stop thinking of God as having a fragile ego or as being vengeful, judgmental, or selective in His favorites. In fact, there's no more His or Her at all. God is love. God is joy. God is compassion. God is the life force that drives every human, plant, and animal.

The issue with the word 'God' is that we've associated that word with a humanlike creature that has magical superpowers. While I'm no student of religion, I loved learning about Greek mythology when I was in college. Instead of one god that looked and acted like a human, there were lots of different gods with both humanlike and godlike qualities. And they were a wild bunch with emotions that were out of control. They were jealous, vengeful, lustful—you name it. But there were so many gods that people didn't look up to them as their maker. Folks were just doing their best to honor them and avoid making them angry.

So farmers had rituals that honored the plant god or the rain god in order to have good crops. Sailors followed rituals to please gods for smooth sailing, like the god of the wind or the god of the sea. And when people wanted to have a baby, they worshiped the goddess of fertility.

Somewhere in history, someone invented the idea of the one-and-only god. And of course, this one-and-only god looked and acted just like a man. Worse, this god was presented as "our father," so now we had a deeply personal connection with this god and all the parental issues that come along with it.

Suddenly, people who now believed in the one-and-only god found themselves trying to please just one god rather than a group of gods. No longer was there a god who controlled the wind or a god who controlled the crops. Now every little thing was controlled by one god. So if your house was wiped out by a tornado, you no longer thought that the wind god was having a temper tantrum because the sun god did something to make him upset. No, now you felt that *you* did something to anger the one-and-only god, who had now leveled your house as punishment.

And that's the heart of the issue for most people. Whenever something goes wrong, "our father" is responsible for all of our suffering. He either caused the tragedy, struggle, or suffering, or at the very least, He allowed it.

So when a person is diagnosed with cancer, that person is now wondering if God gave them cancer as a punishment for something they did or if He allowed the cancer because He just wasn't paying attention. Was God too distracted by His favorites—the celebrities or those who go to church every Sunday—to notice the cancer cells and stop them? Or does God just not care enough about this person to save them from cancer? Now that the one-and-only god has been presented as "our father," we've given Him the power to protect and heal us. And so our life is dependent upon where we stand in the eyes of God when this is our perspective of God.

It's no wonder I couldn't answer the question "Where is God when tragedy and terror strike?" for so many years. I was thinking of God as a person. But all my research into the afterlife found no evidence of such an all-powerful father figure. Certainly, most of the people who had near-death experiences hadn't seen God the father. They saw spirits of all sorts. They felt the presence of God. But none of them could tell me what God looked like. Moreover, those who claimed to have experienced God's *presence* all described God as energy, not an entity. In fact, God to these people was so expansive and infinite that they preferred the terms 'Source,' 'Universe,' 'Creative Intelligence,' 'Oneness,' and even 'Ultimate Love' over the word 'God.'

The same was true for my investigation into spirit communication. Much of this came from readings with mediums. Many of my own loved ones who are now in spirit described God to me as the intelligence of the universe, not some guy in the sky. I now have had hundreds of readings with mediums and seen hundreds of other people have readings with mediums, and never has any spirit come through saying that God is anything other than creative intelligence—the oneness that connects everything.

So how do we view God as anything but human? How do we view God as energy? I honestly think that it's easier if we refrain from using the word altogether. So for the remainder of this book, I'm mostly going to refer to God as Source, the Universe, Universal Energy, or Creative Intelligence. By using those phrases, it's easier to stop thinking of the one-and-only god and to begin thinking in terms of energy rather than entity.

Occasionally, throughout this book, I will throw the word 'God' into a sentence, and you'll see how it trips your mind up a little bit. When I do that, you'll know that it's a little reminder from me of the importance of this paradigm shift. Pause to see how it makes you think and feel. You might be surprised at how entrenched this one-and-only god paradigm is on your psyche. But when you truly break free of it, you'll begin to feel a new sense of inner peace that you never knew was possible.

When I personally recognized this paradigm shift from entity to energy, thousands of little lightbulbs lit up in my brain, and the many questions I had about God and the afterlife were finally given light. That was years ago, but it took me several more years to finally write this book because I wanted to be sure I could articulate my newfound insights before translating them to words. But now it's done.

—⚶—

What's the best way to understand the afterlife?

This is such an important question that it has become the foundation of everything I teach. To state it in a sentence, the best way to understand the afterlife is through personal experience. What this means is that you will come to understand the afterlife much better by having personal experiences rather than listening to a lecture, watching a documentary, or reading a book about other people's experiences.

Personal experience is where we proactively go out and have an experience that involves all or most of our senses. This might be getting a reading of spirit communication with a medium, having a past-life regression with a hypnotic regressionist, or having an out-of-body experience at the Monroe Institute. This might also involve having an experience that does not involve a practitioner, such as doing daily meditation, visiting a spiritual place like Machu Picchu, or practicing inspired writing. The key is that we are actively involved in these personal experiences as opposed to hearing, watching, or reading about someone else's experience vicariously.

Vicarious experience is where most of us begin our spiritual journeys—by learning about the experiences of others. We learn vicariously through other people's stories, books, lectures, workshops, sermons, online videos, websites, TV shows, documentaries, feature films, and the like. Listening to someone talk about her near-death experience is a vicarious spiritual experience. When someone tells us about their experience, we can't touch it, taste it, smell it, or see it with our eyes. We can only imagine that experience in our minds.

It's more advantageous to personally experience a past life during a hypnotic regression (personal experience) than have a psychic tell you about one of your past lives in a reading (vicarious experience). One is a direct multisensory experience; the other is something you must imagine. And direct personal experiences are the only path from believing (where we accept what someone else tells us is true) to knowing (where we know from personal experience that something is true).

You might be wondering how a reading with a medium is a personal experience rather than a vicarious one, especially if you've never had one. This is actually one of those experiences that could fall either way. What makes mediumship a personal experience is that it is a conversation with your loved ones in spirit. So even though a medium is conveying the messages and you can't hear or see your loved one, you are having a personal experience because the messages coming through cause you to have an emotional, visceral experience.

When a stranger tells you accurate information from your loved one in spirit that they could not possibly know, you are affected mentally, emotionally, and physically because you know these messages are coming from your deceased loved one. If you're not affected in this way, the reading might fall more on the side of a vicarious experience.

Now vicarious experiences have precious benefits too. I've learned a great deal from interviewing people who have had near-death experiences. In fact, these interviews have helped me fill in the details whenever my personal experiences only gave me the big picture. The insights gained from those who have had NDEs and ADCs (after-death communications) are priceless, so I'm not suggesting they don't have their place when investigating the afterlife—they most certainly do. But interviews, lectures, books, and documentaries are unable to get one to a "knowing," which is why I recommend personal experience so highly if you want to learn about the afterlife.

I recognized early on in my investigation of the afterlife that I was being taken down a path through three stages. The first stage was where I began, which I call the path of the skeptic. In this stage, I was skeptical because I lacked evidence, so I chose to believe in nothing until I found evidence to believe otherwise.

Then I progressed to the path of the believer. Here, in the believing stage, we accept as truth the beliefs of other people. This is where religion resides because people believe what their religious leaders teach them as true. And this is the stage that comes from vicarious experience. It's a valuable stage in itself and is the only stage that some people ever realize. But it's also a stepping-stone toward personal experience because it teaches us the possibilities for personal experience. If we don't know what to look for, we might never see it when it crosses our path.

At some point along my journey, I stretched into the path of the knower—I *knew* at a deeper level the answers to my spiritual questions in relation to that particular experience. And this knowing was true for me even when my "knowing" was in conflict with what other people claimed was true. And what I realized once I attained my first knowing is that knowing can only come from personal experience.

So skepticism comes from a refusal to believe. Belief comes from vicarious experience. And knowing comes from personal experience.

When I experienced knowing for the first time, it felt more like a remembering than a learning of something new. I guess some people might say that this was the beginning of my spiritual awakening.

I relate this transition from believer to knower as similar to the transition from believing you can ride a bicycle (while your mom or dad holds on to it) to suddenly realizing they are no longer holding on to the bike and you are actually doing it on your own. In its own way, riding a bike is a knowing. You can't fake it. And once you truly "know" how to ride a bicycle, you never forget it—the knowing stays with you forever.

What's most interesting about *knowing* is that one doesn't go from skeptic to believer to knower about all the secrets of the universe at once. Just because we learn to ride a bicycle doesn't mean we now know how to drive a car or fly a plane. We become knowers in fragments, one personal experience at a time.

We can be a knower about one subject while being a skeptic or believer about another. In fact, most everyone is a skeptic about some ideas, a believer about others, and a knower about, still, other ideas.

I once had a respected medium tell me that people who believe in extraterrestrials are naïve. So he was a knower about spirit communication, but a skeptic about ETs. I'm sure there are other folks who believe in extraterrestrials but don't believe that mediums can really communicate with spirits.

Depending upon the subject in question, some people begin in the believer stage, skipping the skeptic stage altogether. My wife, Melissa, never questioned the idea of an afterlife or that it is possible for some people to communicate with spirits. That was never me. I've always been skeptical until gaining some evidence that led me forward. So like Melissa, some people skip skepticism and start off as believers—depending upon the subject.

After months of researching spirit communication, I eventually came to a knowing that we don't die—that there really is life after death. I didn't know exactly what the afterlife experience is like so early in my investigation—I didn't have all the details—but I knew at a cellular level that we survive death. And my transformation from believer to knower in this regard was life changing.

What's wonderful is that the state of knowing is available to anyone. My journey into knowing (regarding certain subjects) is nothing special; that is, it doesn't make me exceptional or extraordinary. To brag about knowing would be the equivalent of bragging about eating. We all can do it. Just because someone hasn't ever thought about it, had the desire to reach knowing, or discovered how to arrive at knowing for some particular subject doesn't make the person who is a knower better than them. Anyone can do it if it's his or her desire.

There is also no one path to knowing. My personal journey of investigating life after death is just *one* way to do it out of infinite possibilities. You get to have whatever personal experience you choose in order to gain a knowing about whatever spiritual subject interests you.

One might refer to a person's knowing as their truth. But my knowing is only my truth. It isn't your truth or anyone else's. So we all have our own truth.

This is not to say that there isn't a single truth—one universal truth—but being human, we can only know truth from our own individual filters. This is related to the "true but not accurate" concept I discussed in the introduction. Our brain functions, past experiences, beliefs, and education all filter our present experiences in a manner that affects our interpretation of each experience and, therefore, our ultimate knowing. That doesn't make one person right and another person wrong, of course; it makes your knowing and my knowing both perfect, even if they are miles apart.

This also means that your truth today might change tomorrow if you have new experiences that add to your knowing. It doesn't make yesterday's knowing wrong; it merely adds a new layer to it, a layer that deepens your understanding at the knowing level. So your knowing today might be different than it was last year in that your level of understanding now allows you to see a bigger picture than you did before. While this can be frustrating information for people who want everything to be in black and white, it's just the way knowing and truth work.

The human challenge is to find our way through life without being born with all the answers. But we have the capacity to learn them, at least many of them. With enough personal experiences, we can eventually gain a knowing that gives us a pretty good picture of what those answers are. And our vicarious experiences can at least fill in the empty spaces with beliefs that satisfy us.

What happens with personal experience is actually quite astounding—you begin to have answers about life, death, and spirituality that you didn't learn through vicarious means. And what you realize is that you gained a knowing during the past-life regression or out-of-body experience or life-between-lives regression that came between the spaces of what you consciously experienced.

In other words, you learned more than you were even consciously aware of learning while having that experience. Suddenly, your questions about life's purpose or why bad things happen to good people or the reason for divine coincidences are just there—you suddenly *know* the answers. And with this knowing comes a deep sense of inner peace. And this is what spiritual growth is all about.

Since this book can only provide you with vicarious beliefs, what I'm trying to inspire you to do is go out and have your own personal experiences toward knowing. Think of this book as a manual of sorts—a map—that opens your awareness about life after death and the possibilities. In other words, become your own investigator. With this, you can pursue new spiritual experiences toward knowing with greater confidence and mindfulness. Then one day, the answers about life and death will come from within you as a knowing. And that is a most peaceful and joyful place to be.

PART TWO

—⁂—

QUESTIONS ABOUT DEATH AND DYING

What determines how and when we die?

Throughout this book, keep in mind that my using the word 'die' has a slightly different meaning than how most people use it. Dying, when I use the word, only means that our physical body dies, not our consciousness. In reality, we go on living without our body—consciousness survives death. So when I use the word 'die' (or 'dying') in this book, I'm simply referring to the death of the physical body. When this occurs, our spirit (consciousness) returns to the spirit world (the afterlife).

There are multiple factors that determine how and when we die. I'll explain five of the key factors here, but keep in mind that there are an infinite number of factors. It's important to know too that while one or two factors might be the most influential, it's really an intricate combination and balance of them all that leads to the ultimate deciding factor.

PRE-BIRTH CHOICES: The first factor consists of our pre-birth choices regarding what we came into this lifetime to accomplish. Picture yourself as a soul in the spirit world (before you are born) getting together with your spirit guides to help preplan your trip to the physical plane (this human life). You and your guides decide that there are particular experiences you want to have, meaning you want to gain certain lessons and insights that can only be obtained by having a human life. Well, once you have completed what you came to experience in your lifetime, it's eventually going to be time for you to leave this life and go back home to the spirit world. But this is just one factor of many.

It's also possible that your soul recognizes that you won't be able to accomplish all that you hoped to experience here. This too happens. It's not terribly disappointing or uncommon for a soul to realize that some of its goals just aren't going to happen—it just is. But recognizing this can be a determining factor in your soul's choice to end your lifetime. It's like, "Okay, I've completed all the goals that I'm going to be able to complete. Do I have any other reasons to stick around?"

LIFE ENJOYMENT: Having said what I did about pre-birth choices, many souls choose to hang around and enjoy life for a while once they've accomplished what they desired to experience in this lifetime. As we know, all work and no play makes Jack a dull boy, so it's not like everyone instantly dies the moment they finish what they came here to do. While some souls will choose to leave quickly, some souls like to exit life slowly and gradually, what we might think of as dying of old age. And of course, we always continue to learn and grow from a spiritual perspective, even if we have already completed the major experiences we hoped to know in our lifetime.

ASSISTING OTHERS: Some souls choose to remain on the physical plane in order to help other souls accomplish what they set out to experience during their lifetimes. It's not all about us, although we do gain from helping others. No other soul "needs" us in order to accomplish what they set out to experience here (there are multiple opportunities for them to accomplish their own goals), but if we can be helpful, we might choose to stick around for the benefit of another.

OPPORTUNITY: Another factor that determines how and when we die is opportunity. If we take into account that our spirit guides (including our soul self, otherwise known as our higher self) are forever creating miracles and coincidences for our benefit, it helps to understand that an opportunity might arrive for us to exit the planet—that is, if we've completed what we came here to do or know that we will not be able to complete what we came here to do.

Say, for example, that the potential for a car accident crosses our path. In this case, our spirit guides and soul determine if this is the best moment for us to exit our human life. If it is, the accident happens, and our life is over. If it's not, we might not get in the accident at all, or we might be involved in the accident but are not killed in it, possibly not even injured.

While there are infinite factors that determine the time, place, and circumstances of one's death, opportunity is an important factor. Yet opportunity can be affected by one's free will, the next factor described below.

FREE WILL: One of the most important factors that determine how and when we die is free will. Most people have no idea just how powerful our free will is. I have a friend whose mother was dying in her home on New Year's Eve. The 90-year-old woman's organs were shutting down, and everyone knew death was imminent. In accordance with her personality, hours before midnight, the dying woman asked her husband if it was more advantageous for their tax return if she died on December 31 or January 1. He looked it up online and found that it was better if she passed after the New Year had begun. Sure enough, the dying woman clung to life and took her last breath at 12:10 a.m.

So free will plays a critical role in how and when we die. If, for instance, a person purposely takes their own life, it was free will that ended that life. If a person suddenly takes a left turn instead of going straight as planned, that freewill choice might avoid the fatal accident.

If a person chooses to treat their illness alternatively by eating raw foods, practicing self-love, and spending more time with loved ones (and less time working), that person might heal the illness that was going to end their life. Why? That person's soul might recognize a valuable experience is in the works that the soul would benefit from experiencing.

Our pre-birth choices, life enjoyment, assisting others, opportunity, and free will are just some of the significant factors that determine how and when we die, but there are an infinite number of factors at stake. Since our deaths also affect many other people (people who love and depend upon us or people we don't know who might be affected in some way by our deaths), there is a lot going on behind the scenes regarding the decision to end our life—infinite factors that must be taken into account. Since our spirit guides and soul self can understand all these infinite factors much better than we can, these factors are all taken into account and factored into the final determination of how and when we die.

—⚹—

When does our spirit leave our body at death?

Our soul (higher self) is really in charge of this choice, and a lot depends upon what our soul wants to experience. Since the purpose of life is to have experiences that can only be known in physical form—including both positive and negative experiences—our soul might or might not feel any benefit from going through a particular dying experience. While our own personal free will does play a large part in how we die, it is our soul that ultimately decides when to pull our spirit out of our body. And when the spirit leaves, the suffering stops.

Many people in spirit have communicated through mediums that their spirit left their body before the airplane or automobile crashed, before the bullet hit their body, and before the pain of any death experience got unbearable. When this occurs, we experience our death while out of our body, yet we are still connected to it spiritually.

Many people who have had near-death experiences have also said that they left their body seconds before the physical impact of whatever nearly killed them.

On the other hand, some souls want to know what a particular death experience is like in order to truly know it. Why might a soul desire this? This experience allows that soul to gain compassion for people going through that same experience (or one similar to it).

For example, a soul might want to experience starving to death or dying from a particular terminal illness. While this might seem absurd from our human point of view, the spiritual view is that life is about experiences, and any specific type of death is an experience that teaches us something that is valuable to our eternal spiritual growth.

If we stop to consider why a soul chooses to experience a physical lifetime in the first place, a lot of it has to do with the fact that human lives end. Our mortality is something we as souls cannot experience in the spirit world because our existence there is eternal. Yet the fact that we can die affects many of our choices and ignites many of our fears. So it's valuable for souls to experience mortality because it teaches them so much that they are unable to learn or know in the afterlife.

To add just little more depth to this answer, karma is one of the many reasons a soul might want to undergo a particular dying experience. If, for example, a soul had a lifetime that involved shooting people to their deaths, that soul might want to know the experience of being shot to death in order to gain new compassion for its victims in that other lifetime. It's not about balance or punishment; it's about the soul seeing the experience from both sides—being the shooter and being shot.

This can happen in the opposite way too. A soul that had a lifetime as a doctor helping people with diseases—diseases that slowly deteriorate the body until death—might want to experience such a disease to gain a new level of understanding for how he helped those patients and perhaps to gain a new level of compassion for people suffering with these diseases.

So your spirit might leave your body at some point before death. Or your spirit might remain in your body in order to experience everything right up until the moment that your physical body dies. Still, even if your spirit stays up to the last minute, the comforting news is that the second your spirit leaves your body, there's no more pain, no more fear, and no more suffering in relation to your body. You have separated from your physical essence, and all the pain and suffering is instantly gone.

—∿—

Why do the dying often wait until their loved ones leave the room before they pass?

It's often very difficult for surviving family members and friends to understand why their loved ones died while they were out of the room for only a brief period of time or died only minutes or hours before they arrived to be with them.

Our soul, which is that part of us that remains in the spirit world while our spirit inhabits a physical body, ultimately decides our time of death. So, for instance, if a person's soul knows that she is more likely to hang on to life and resist crossing over into the afterlife while loved ones are in the room with her, that soul will influence death while those loved ones have temporarily left the room (perhaps to go eat or talk to the doctor) or before those loved ones arrive in the first place.

Alternatively, if one's soul knows that a family member is not emotionally equipped to be present at the time of their death, the soul will influence death when that family member has left the room (or before that family member arrives)—possibly in cooperation with that family member's spirit guides.

This is often a confusing and sometimes frustrating occurrence to people who are in grief. I've heard many ask, "Why did she die when I was only out of the room for five minutes?" While the answer to that question has infinite possibilities, it's important to simply trust that there is a reason. And it's important to keep in mind that the reason might have been for the benefit of the person dying too. So we must trust that it happened for someone's benefit, and we must not feel hurt or cheated by this soul's final decision while in this body.

Soul decisions aside, dying alone can also be an intentional act of free will on the part of the dying person—the human being. There are many people who, for the sake of pride and dignity, prefer to die alone. There are all sorts of involuntary bodily functions that can occur at death, and these might seem embarrassing to a dying person. Or the dying person might think it's best for their loved ones, even if the loved ones wouldn't agree. In these cases, the dying are exercising their own free will to determine their time of death. And it's important that we respect their final choice with grace as it might have been their last act of free will.

—ɷ—

Is death painful?

It's helpful to make a distinction between the word 'dying' and the word 'death.' Dying (a physical event) can be painful. Death (a spiritual event) is not.

Death is the state where you are physically dead, but your consciousness survives. Many people who have died for a few seconds or minutes and then been revived have said that they were fully aware of their body and surroundings while dead, only they were not in their bodies during these experiences. These are called near-death experiences (NDEs).

For many, the initial stage of the NDE is called an out-of-body experience (OBE). In many cases during near-death experiences, people found themselves floating up by the ceiling above everyone else in the room (for example, above the doctors in the emergency room). If they were outdoors when they died, they floated freely above their body. Many who have had this experience said the transition was natural: "One second, I was running for shelter across a field during a lightning storm. The next second, I was floating above my body as it lay on the grass."

Regardless of the state of their physical bodies, there was never any pain felt while floating in this observer position separated from their bodies. Even those who were struck by lightning or hit by a train, for instance, had no sensation other than weightlessness, freedom from the confines of their dense physical body, and a deep sense of inner peace. Most people who have experienced these near-death experiences admit that they felt so absolutely wonderful while out of their body that they did not want to return to it. That's how blissful it feels to leave our bodies and exist in spiritual form.

Of course, anyone living who has told us about their near-death experience (NDE) obviously did return to their body, and that is when they felt the pain of the harrowing experience that caused them to leave their body for a brief time in the first place, if there is any pain associated with the experience that caused the NDE.

While I defined NDEs and OBEs earlier in this book, it's important to know that these terms are not synonymous. Many people have had out-of-body experiences without being near death. In fact, some people have learned that they can intentionally leave their body so that their consciousness travels around while their body remains stationary.

Just as commonly, folks who have had near-death experiences have not always hovered over their body to observe it. These near-death experiencers instantly found themselves in some spiritual realm upon leaving their bodies, completely skipping the stage of seeing their body altogether.

—ɯ—

Is death scary?

Once again, while dying can be scary for most people due to fear of the unknown, death itself is not scary. Those who have died and returned to tell us about it say that they felt nothing but love, warmth, and inner peace during their near-death experience. And once they left the vicinity of their physical bodies and gravitated toward the brilliant light of the afterlife, these feelings of love, joy, peace, and safety grew more intense the closer they got to the light. Then once they entered the light (what some call heaven or the spirit world), they were indescribably steeped in these blissful feelings.

There are some near-death experiencers who described one point where they felt fear. It was at the moment when they were floating above their body and realized that no one around them was aware of them. Imagine being in the room at the moment of your death. People are looking at your physical body and saying that you're dead, but you're there trying to tell them, "I'm not dead. I'm right over here. Just look up toward the ceiling. I'm still alive." Yet nobody hears or sees you.

This is the point where some people reported feeling fear. Yet the exact moment that these people became fearful is the moment when a spiritual being came into their awareness. And just as swiftly as this spiritual guide, angel, or being of light appeared, their fear disappeared. Furthermore, the closer this spiritual being got to them, the more comfort, love, peace, and security they felt. So even in these cases, the fear lasted only for a very brief moment before it was replaced with feelings of safety and tranquility.

—⁂—

Is death dark?

Some people might describe death as dark, but death is not dark in the way that we know darkness. In the darkness of our physical world, we can't see anything—it is total blackness. As a result, our darkness can be frightening because we don't know what is before us. Evidence indicates that this is not true of the spirit world.

The most compelling evidence of this comes, once again, from near-death experiences (NDEs). Many people who have had NDEs describe their initial transition into this alternate dimension as being in darkness but say that there is light within the darkness. Rather than describe a frightening blackness, they experienced a soothing darkness that illuminated whatever was within it. They added that it was a comforting, peaceful darkness because they could still see in it. One near-death experiencer described it to me as a soft velvety darkness where light radiated wherever she focused her attention. Others who have had NDEs told me that they agreed with that description considering human words can only be so accurate.

Other people who have experienced NDEs described the initial act of leaving their physical bodies as traveling through a dark tunnel. However, in her book *Near-Death Experiences: The Rest of the Story*, NDE researcher P. M. H. Atwater says that the tunnel experience is actually quite rare. Her findings indicate that many people say they had a tunnel experience (when they didn't) because they worry people won't believe they had a near-death experience without adding the "tunnel" experience into their story.

My investigation has led me to believe that the experience that people are having is vaguely similar, but not exactly like a tunnel. Like all spiritual experiences, what they actually experienced is so difficult to describe in human terms that the "tunnel" is the easiest way to describe it, even though that description is not precisely accurate.

Many people who attempted to illustrate their tunnel experience said the tunnel had beautiful lights and colors within it (some said on the walls of it), and the bright light of the spirit world was at the end of that tunnel, which they traveled toward without any effort on their part (they were drawn to the light naturally). And the closer they got to this light, the more they felt the love, joy, peace, and security of the bright, luminous spirit world.

So this darkness seems to have no resemblance to what we know as darkness. It's probably more accurate to describe it as a muted or vacant visual that illuminates only those beings who are present—or whatever we happen to focus upon.

It's important to remember that near-death experiences (which are a temporary death) are not entirely the same as the experience of being permanently dead (never coming back into your physical body).

Of course, I'm using the word 'dead' the way the general public uses it. Anyone who is reading this book quickly learns that we don't really die; we merely transition to another dimension—the spiritual dimension, which is eternal.

But the point I'm making here is that a near-death experience is only a glimpse of the spirit world. It is not the same experience as being a spirit in the spirit world who will not be returning to her physical body. So people who have had NDEs cannot tell us exactly what the spirit world is like for our deceased loved ones in spirit because near-death experiencers are sent back to their human bodies before they get very far. Therefore, we must consider other evidence that helps us answer this question about death being dark.

People in spirit who have communicated through mediums and people who have communicated with spirits during their deathbed visions have described the light of the spiritual dimension as being 100 times brighter than the sun, yet it never hurts their eyes (no sunglasses necessary).

Just imagine sitting on a beach in the warm sun and soaking in the rays on your skin. According to these spirits, this imagery barely touches upon the actual magnificence of the light of the spirit world as there are no human words that can fully describe it with any sense of accuracy and justice. Yet despite the fact that words don't exist to properly describe it, I think we all get the idea that the spirit world offers a brilliant and wonderful luminosity that is nothing like the darkness that we know here on the earth plane and probably nothing like the darkness of the early NDE stages either.

My conclusions are that the velvety darkness that has light within it is what we experience during our transition back home to the spirit world. But it's not frightening in any way but rather beautiful and comforting. And perhaps this helps us to recognize and be drawn toward the luminous light of the spirit world, which is our final destination.

—⚹—

Do we continue to feel our pain, sickness, or sadness after death?

To be in spirit form means to be free of all physical suffering. This means we do not feel pain, and all our maladies, injuries, and deformities are healed, both physical and mental. This means that even depression, mania, and dementia are nonexistent in spirit. As spirits, we are perfectly whole and healthy.

If you are missing an arm, leg, or eye in this lifetime, you won't be once you return to the spirit world. If you walk with a limp, you'll walk perfectly in spirit. If your back is in chronic pain, it will feel pain-free in spirit. If you talk with a stutter, have obsessive-compulsive disorder, or twitch from Tourette's syndrome, you won't in spirit.

The only caveat here is that we can be anything we want in spirit. So when you die in this lifetime and return home to the spirit world, you will get whatever you want and expect once you're there. All you have to do is think of something, and it becomes your reality.

Consequently, after you immediately cross over to the other side, if you still think of yourself as missing your left index finger, then you might experience yourself in spirit as missing your left index finger. Yet all you have to do is think of yourself as perfect and whole, and—*boom*, done—you'll instantly have all 10 fingers. Change your thought, and your reality changes. And this is true for any conditions we might expect to have, which is why having books like this to prepare you for the afterlife can be really handy. You'll be way ahead of the game when you get there because you won't have to learn by trial and error as so many people have done.

I'll explain this more in upcoming answers, but for now, I must add that we don't have physical bodies in the spirit world. We are beings of light. That is our true nature, which is why we do not carry any of our human suffering into the afterlife. So we have the ability to feel as if we still have a physical body—if that is something we feel we need in our transition back to the spirit world—but before long, we settle into our lightness of being and exist as spiritual beings, not physical beings. Once we settle into our true spiritual essence, we don't experience ourselves as having physical bodies at all.

—⚍—

Will I remember who I am and what I'm like in the afterlife?

You will definitely remember everything about your life in the spirit world, even more than you might want to remember. Everything that you ever said, did, or thought is recalled, mostly due to a process we go through upon our entry back into the spirit world known as our life review. While I'll cover this in more detail in another section of this book, suffice it to say that you will have the opportunity to reexamine all of your choices and actions in this lifetime in order to evaluate and learn from them.

The truth is that you'll know and understand yourself better once you're in spirit than you currently do. With our transition from the physical to the spiritual comes clarity—clarity regarding our personality traits and characteristics, our choices and actions, and even how we affected other people and the world. Plus the life review process especially helps us to know who we were in our human life with a depth of insight we just don't have as human beings.

There is a purpose for living a physical life, so remembering everything about who we are is part of the process—it's the reason for having a human life. Who we are and how we live our lives will stay with us for all eternity, which is why every day of our lives is so important. This is a great reminder while we're alive so that we can make the most out of life and be the best person we know how to be. After all, the memories of this lifetime are everlasting.

—ᘏᘏ—

If our brain is dead, how can we be conscious after death?

Contrary to common belief, our minds are not an aspect of our brains. No doctor or scientist has ever dissected a brain and found the mind, otherwise known as consciousness. This is why many people who have had near-death experiences (and were determined to be brain-dead at a hospital) were able to see and hear everything the doctors were doing and saying during the time they were pronounced dead. Our minds are spiritual-based and therefore not a physical component of our brains, which is why our conscious minds survive death.

There's actually no distinction between our consciousness and our spirit. So in this way, I'm using the words 'consciousness,' 'spirit,' and 'mind' in the same way. On the other hand, some people use the word 'mind' to mean "brain function." This is not an accurate depiction of the way I'm referring to the mind.

Our brain function controls our body movements, directs how we relate to our physical environment, and even determines whether we're going to be good at math, English, or music. Our consciousness, from a spiritual perspective, is good at everything. But it's a fine line that separates brain function and the conscious mind, which is why many doctors and scientists once believed the two were one and the same.

For all intents and purposes, brain function and conscious mind are the same while we're living in a physical body because our brain function affects our consciousness while in the body. For example, mental illness and learning disabilities affect how we think and act, so these brain functions limit our consciousness while in the body—the brain's ability to function filters our consciousness. But the moment we die, our conscious mind separates from our brain just as our spirit separates from our body. Everything that is physical (body and brain) stops. Everything that is spiritual (spirit and consciousness) continues. In actuality, as mentioned, the words 'spirit' and 'consciousness' are synonymous.

When we die and leave our bodies, we are only consciousness—the same consciousness we had while in our physical bodies, although with much greater awareness because the brain no longer filters our clarity. Once we are no longer confined by our physical limitations (which includes our brain and its functions) and we return to the afterlife, our awareness expands to greater spiritual knowing, which is our natural, eternal state.

—⚏—

My loved one was talking or seeing someone in spirit hours before he died. What was happening?

It's common that dying people are welcomed by their loved ones in spirit days or hours before their death. These experiences are known as deathbed visions or pre-death visions. I actually prefer the term 'pre-death visions,' but I use 'deathbed visions' in this book because it's the more commonly used term.

Deathbed visions are when loved ones in spirit visit a dying person days or hours before their death in order to welcome them back to the spirit world. In this way, the dying are greeted by deceased family members and friends (even pets) to prepare them for their forthcoming transition from human to spirit and thereby ease any fears or anxiety they might have about death.

In most deathbed visions, the dying person will see or hear (often both) their deceased loved ones on the other side. Some describe this experience as their loved ones letting them know that they won't be alone when the time comes to make the transition.

It's common that these conversations can last for several minutes at a time and happen several times a day. Sometimes the people in spirit aren't talking, but the dying person recognizes that they are present in the room. Usually, when there is communication from spirit to human, it happens telepathically (by thought)—from spirit to human *and* human to spirit—so no words need to be spoken out loud.

To visitors who are in the room when this takes place, it can seem like their dying loved one is hallucinating. And of course, some doctors and nurses erroneously believe that's what's happening. To witnesses, the messages the dying person is getting might appear lucid and cohesive, while at other times, they might seem disjointed and erratic. This often creates confusion among family members as to whether their dying loved one is experiencing dementia or true spirit contact.

Regardless of how it might seem to witnesses in the room, the communication from spirit always comes through clearly to the person receiving it. And it is such a wonderful gift to the dying that eases their fears and reduces their anxiety around death that it should always be welcomed and accepted.

I should note too that family or friends who are visiting and are in the room when a deathbed vision takes place sometimes share the experience. So don't be surprised if you are visiting a dying loved one in the hospital, for instance, and all of a sudden you sort of go into a dreamlike state and share the experience that your dying loved one is experiencing. This is called a shared-deathbed vision and can be quite beautiful and comforting.

Some people have even had shared-death experiences, where they witness their loved one leaving their body and going to the spirit world. How cool is that? This too is a dreamlike experience that only lasts a brief moment. But it can also be quite comforting and reassuring to loved ones left behind because they get a glimpse of where their deceased loved one has gone.

—ᘯᘯ—

What happens to people who are sedated by morphine when they die?

The only thing that changes when people are sedated by morphine or other drugs while dying is that they might not be awake to have a *conscious* deathbed vision, but they are likely still being met by loved ones in spirit in their unconscious state.

So deathbed visions are much more common when hospital and hospice patients are not sedated by morphine, but that makes sense considering the dying patient is not conscious to tell anyone about it. If they can't tell someone about their pre-death experience, deathbed vision researchers can't record the incident as a statistic.

Nonetheless, painkilling drugs are not affecting what happens after people die and leave their bodies. Just like people who die on the operating table while under anesthesia or people who die from a drug overdose, the drugs have absolutely no effect on their conscious minds once they've separated from their bodies. They feel absolutely no effects from the sedating drug once in spirit because their spirits are free from all physical sensations of the body. So the morphine does not affect their transition back to spirit.

—⁓—

What can I do to help my loved one's transition into the spirit world?

Our loved ones don't need our assistance when crossing over to the other side. The process happens unconsciously and instinctively, just like birth, yet even more flawlessly. While we humans have learned to control the birth process in order to reduce complications, women were practicing natural childbirth long before we had hospitals. Even if you've never witnessed a natural birth, if you've ever watched a cat or dog give birth, you know what I'm talking about. There are some natural processes that work just fine without human interference, and death is one of them.

It's important you understand that you don't hold the responsibility of your loved one's transition back to the spirit world on your shoulders, but feel free to pray for their smooth and peaceful transition. It's always a kind and supportive gesture to pray for another. All you have to do is send them love. There are many people who have had near-death experiences who claim to have seen the light of prayers passing by them in the spirit world like little energy beams of love, which they were told can be quite beneficial to their recipients.

So prayers are not necessary, but they are quite beneficial. Still, there are other things you can do to help your loved one who has passed.

Our loved ones feel our grief in the spirit world, so it pains them to see our suffering due to their loss. In order to help your recently deceased loved one, treat yourself with love and kindness by stepping up your self-care regimen. Surround yourself with supportive loved ones who can be there for you in body, mind, and spirit. And if at all possible, see a grief counselor who resonates with your personality.

Keep in mind that grief should never be rushed as it's an important process of experiencing loss. Nor should it be denied. There's nothing weak about mourning the death of a loved one. Bereavement is a natural process and an experience that benefits the evolution of your soul. Even animals express sorrow due to loss. So be gentle with yourself over the coming months and years following your loved one's death. It will help them to know you are getting the proper care and support.

At the same time, don't be hard on yourself for what you could have done better or should have done when your loved one was alive. It's good to learn from your mistakes, but it helps no one when you beat yourself up about your regrets. Forgive yourself for whatever mistakes you made or things you could have improved, and move forward. I have never heard a person in spirit say they didn't immediately forgive their loved ones for everything that was said or done. They always forgive. And they suffer along with you if you are being too hard on yourself for something of this nature following their passing. So do it for yourself, and do it for them.

This does not mean that you get to treat others who are still alive just as poorly as you treated the deceased. And it is by no means a free ticket for you to abuse others by thinking you'll be forgiven by them in spirit. Rather, a person's passing is an opportunity for you to learn from your mistakes and become a better person by never repeating that mistreatment, abuse, or wrongdoing. If you truly transform yourself by recognizing the errors of your ways (knowing that you can't fool spirit), you will be forgiven and supported during your transformation into the person your soul hoped to be in this lifetime.

Furthermore, please know that your loved one does not want or expect you to grieve forever either. The bereavement process is for your sake, not the deceased. While our loved ones in spirit appreciate being remembered, your never-ending mourning does not honor them. Quite the opposite is true. Since they can feel your anguish, it troubles them to see you suffering. So don't hang on to your sorrow for their sake. Grieve as long as is necessary, but not longer.

In a story related to this question, I was recently with a close friend who had lost her husband about a year prior. He was only 38 years old when he passed. In an exercise of spirit communication, the wife asked her husband if there was anything she could do for him. His answer came through quickly and clearly. He said, "Be happy."

—⁘—

Do we instantly know that we're dead when we die?

The simple answer is that some know instantly, and some figure it out rather quickly. In cases where people first have an out-of-body experience and are looking down from above at their body, there is sometimes a bit of a surprise at seeing their lifeless body. Yet this surprise doesn't last long as it doesn't take a rocket scientist to figure out you're dead when you're looking down at your body from above. So it's a very brief moment in most cases before we realize we're no longer alive.

For those who do not have the out-of-body experience where they see their body before them, they generally find themselves in an entry-level place that many have described as a darkness that has light within it, which I previously described. One person I interviewed said it was a peaceful velvety darkness that lit up wherever she focused her attention. Others have some sort of tunnel experience, which varies in description from person to person. Still, others instantly find themselves at the entryway to the spirit world, where all that bright, warm, loving light exists. If you don't know you're dead by this point (which happens in a flash), someone in spirit will tell you because there will be loved ones in spirit, as well as spirit guides, who are waiting to greet you there.

For many people, a spirit guide or deceased loved one in spirit will greet you soon after you've exited your human body and will caringly escort you to the spirit world. In some cases, these nonphysical beings are welcoming you home days or minutes before you've died (deathbed visions) to let you know they will be there when you cross over. Regardless of who greets you, they will let you know that your human life is over if you don't already know, and they'll help you get reacquainted with your spiritual essence.

—⁓—

What happens when a person dies at such an early age that they don't have any deceased loved ones in spirit to greet them?

There are always people in spirit to greet us regardless of how many family members or friends in our current life have died before us.

For one, the spirit world is home to us, so we know a lot more people in spirit than we'll ever know in our human life. Don't forget that we each have spirit guides who helped us plan our life before we were born and then continued to guide our life while we were here. These guides will also be there to greet us home when we return to the spiritual dimension. And of course, we'll recognize them like old friends because we won't be blocked by the veil or curtain of forgetfulness that we have in human form.

Two, it's not uncommon that we meet ancestors of our parents before we're ever born. For instance, before a baby is born, her spirit might meet the spirit of her maternal grandmother who died before that baby's birth. In this way, the spirits of the grandmother and the baby meet before the baby is ever born—before the baby's mother even meets her on the physical plane. That's a mind twister, but it's fun to contemplate. As a result, any relatives who were already in spirit before a person was born will be there to greet that person when they die and come back home again.

Three, we also know people in spirit from other lifetimes. Since we have all lived hundreds or thousands of lives before this one, there are truckloads of people in spirit available to greet us when we return to the afterlife. Although we might not know them from this lifetime, that doesn't mean we won't recognize them when we return. These people in spirit were once our mothers, fathers, children, spouses, siblings, and friends in other lifetimes. As a result, if we live only a day, a year, or a decade, there are always plenty of spirits we know who are ready and waiting for us to cross back over to our true home. And no matter how long it's been, there's always a welcome-back reunion celebration.

Four, if you recall what I wrote at the beginning of this book about souls and spirits, you might remember that our soul always remains in the spirit world. This means that the souls of all our loved ones are back home in the spiritual realm. So if a baby passes before her parents, she will be greeted by the souls of her parents upon her return home. I know this might be hard to grasp, but just think of our souls as our higher selves—that whole-self aspect of us that guides us from the spirit world. With this in mind, the souls of all our loved ones are in spirit, so no one ever dies without anyone to greet them in spirit.

—☽—

Will I be able to communicate with the living after I die?

You will certainly be able to communicate with the living while in spirit, although the messages are subtler than the direct communication we know as humans. I recall more than one time after my father died, for example, that the room I was in suddenly filled with the scent of lilacs, even though all the windows and doors were closed and there were no lilacs in the house or in the yard. This happened to me several times in my house and in my car following my father's passing. Lilacs were my father's favorite flower, so it was just his way of saying hello—letting me know he was alive in spirit and still around me.

Aroma is a common method of communication for people in spirit, especially if they have recently passed. The communication they are attempting to make is that they are present. They want us to know that they are okay, they are not gone, and they are still with us. They are trying to help ease the pain of our grief by sending us the message that they still exist.

There are many ways that we are able to communicate with the living after we've died—which I cover in more detail in another section—but none are more direct than through a reading with a psychic medium (often just called a medium).

In a medium reading, people in spirit can say exactly what they want to say to the living. Sure, it's not a perfectly clear communication as we are used to having, but at least the communication is in words, pictures, and feelings. That's right, the communication comes in sounds that the medium can hear (known as clairaudience), pictures that they can see in their mind's eye (clairvoyance), and feelings that they can feel in their body (clairsentience). Sometimes the communication simply comes to them as a knowing (claircognizance).

In your average one-hour reading with a medium, a person in spirit can usually give you evidence that the medium is linked with them by conveying their appearance (what you remember your loved one in spirit to look like), their approximate age, their profession if they had one or if they were in school, how they passed (car accident, heart attack, suicide), what their personality was like, memories you had together when they were alive, and even some recent past events in your life to prove that they are still aware of what's going on in your life even though they're now in spirit (such as they saw you at their gravesite).

After the person in spirit has been clearly identified by the medium, the spirit generally conveys nonevidential messages, which are messages that do not necessarily provide evidence that the medium is communicating with them but rather are messages of advice, love, pride, and forgiveness. Once you are convinced that the medium is really communicating with your loved one in spirit, these messages have a strong emotional impact.

Of course, when you're in spirit, it might not be easy getting the living to go to a psychic medium. There are a lot of people who are skeptical and even cynical about mediums and spirit communication. I know because I used to be one of those people. That was before I began investigating this field. Still, once in spirit, you'll have some ability to influence your loved ones on the physical plane to get a reading. You might be able to influence them via their intuition. Or you might be able to create some coincidences where you influence a friend or acquaintance of theirs to invite them to a reading or medium demonstration (where a medium gives readings in front of a live audience).

After you have passed and are in spirit, there are no guarantees that your living loved ones will listen to their intuition or their friend's recommendations or invitations. In many cases, people never see a medium, thereby never giving their loved ones in spirit an opportunity to communicate with them in this way. In this case, you'll be limited to other forms of after-death communication, such as spreading scents, flickering lights, making radios or televisions go haywire, or making phones ring (even though no one will be on the other end when they answer).

There's a good chance that your loved ones will view these signals as mere coincidence, which is why awareness about the afterlife is so important. But the greatest obstacle when sending these signals is that you might actually frighten your loved ones while trying to contact them. Thanks to all the TV shows and movies on ghosts and hauntings, your loved ones might not realize it's you attempting to say hello and might instead think it's a ghost trying to scare them. Such is the challenge of after-death communication.

PART THREE

—⚭—

QUESTIONS ABOUT THE AFTERLIFE /
SPIRIT WORLD

What's the difference between the afterlife, heaven, the here-after, the spirit world, and the other side?

These are all different words and phrases for the same concept. In this book, I'll vary my use of these words, but I'll always mean the same thing. Basically, I'm referring to the dimension we go to after we die. I grew up Catholic, so I used to call this place heaven. Today, I'm spiritual without a religious affiliation, so I more commonly use different words like 'the afterlife,' 'the hereafter,' 'the spirit world,' and 'the other side.'

Although some people discuss the afterlife as that place we go after our passing, the spirit world is actually our home base. The physical life we live here on earth is where we visit temporarily, but we always return home to the spirit world.

The word 'afterlife' is technically a little misleading because we are used to thinking in terms of life or death. It suggests that life (physical life on earth) is what comes first, and death (spiritual life on the other side) is what comes second or *after*. In reality, our spiritual existence comes first before we ever have a physical life, so we plan our human life while in the spirit world long before we are born. Consequently, spiritual life does not come "after" life; it actually comes before our human life.

All the same, these are just words, and no harm is done in creating a misnomer. And because these words are so ingrained in our minds, I'm going to continue using them throughout this book, although with little reminders along the way of their true meaning.

Since we're on the subject, I should also note that I will refer to "death" as meaning we are in spirit, even though we are still very much alive in the spirit world. Again, these words are such a normal part of our vocabulary that I feel it's more important that I use the words and phrases that you're used to using rather than give you a new dictionary from which to read this book. As long as you understand that the afterlife is a spiritual existence that actually comes before human life (as well as after it) and that death is a state of being alive in spirit, there's nothing wrong with using these words and phrases.

—m—

Why has no one proven that the afterlife exists?

Most people erroneously use the word 'prove' when talking about the afterlife. The correct word to use is 'evidence.' No one is ever going to prove the afterlife exists to everyone because proof is subjective. This is why we could have two juries look at the same evidence of an alleged criminal, and one jury could say the man is guilty while the other jury could say he is innocent. Because proof is subjective, we can show the same evidence but get two opposite verdicts.

Evidence, on the other hand, is objective. If we have a video of the alleged criminal committing a crime or the gun that shot the victim with the alleged criminal's fingerprints on it, that video and gun are impartial evidence. No one can protest otherwise.

Notwithstanding the objective nature of evidence, however, the degree of weight each piece of evidence holds is also subjective. Said another way, deciding whether the evidence is compelling enough to lead one to believe it's proof is an individual choice. I might suspect that the video had been altered in order to frame the alleged criminal on trial (thereby providing little or no weight as evidence), while someone else could believe that the video was unaltered and, therefore, compelling enough to equal proof (to them) that the person on trial committed the crime.

Since evidence is objective and proof is subjective, no one will ever prove to the masses that an afterlife exists. You can show some people the evidence and they might conclude that the evidence equals proof to them, but there will always be just as many people who are unconvinced by that same evidence.

—⁓—

What's it like in the spirit world?

When we initially cross over to the spirit world after dying, some believe there is a period of transition where our spirits get reacquainted with the spirit world. In this phase, the recently crossed over are said to imagine themselves as they were in their physical lives (human lives) until they get reacclimated to their spirit-world reality.

Since we can do, be, and have anything we desire in the spirit world, imagining their life as it was on earth might become their temporary reality. And from this perceived reality, they might feel like they have a body that seemingly needs food, sleep, shelter, and clothing.

During this early stage of reintegration back into the spiritual realm, some spirits imagine themselves in the last home they knew in their physical life, some imagine being in their childhood homes (because they felt most comfortable and happy there), and some invent the home of their dreams that they could never afford during their physical life. The choice is yours for the making. Wherever you wish to be, whatever you want it to look like, you can have it. Your only limit is your imagination.

Since we can do, be, and have whatever we want in the afterlife, this is also true for what we eat, what we wear, and what we are able to do. Want to drive a Maserati? Want to play a musical instrument? Want to be a talented gymnast? Want to eat chocolate all day and never get fat? Want to dress in Armani? Whatever you want and can imagine, that can be your life in the hereafter.

As good as all of that might seem, my investigation into the afterlife has taught me that imagined realities are not our true nature as spiritual beings. Food, cars, clothing, and houses are possessions of physical beings. Spiritual beings have no interest in such belongings. So once our reentry back home is complete and we've had the opportunity to readjust, our desire for such things disappears.

Moreover, this idea of the transitionary phase for spirits is a subject for debate. If it truly exists, it is likely more for people who haven't learned anything about the afterlife before their physical death—or outright don't believe in it. In these cases, since we get whatever we focus upon in spirit (and whatever we expect), these newly arrived spirits might be holding on to their physical memories and, therefore, experience what they expect to experience—more of the same (more human life).

The other cause for debating the transitionary period is that it implies time is involved, which doesn't exist in the afterlife. So if time doesn't exist in the spirit world, the transitionary period sounds an awful lot like a fictional story that a human made up in an attempt to understand or describe the afterlife. After all, some humans tend to believe (or want to believe) that the spirit world is just like the physical world. As we know, many folks don't like change.

I can also understand why humans would make this assumption if they've had readings with mediums. I've had readings where my relatives in spirit made claims through mediums that they were doing human activities. For example, I had an uncle who told me that he was fishing in the spirit world. Obviously, considering that he's a being of light, his claim is likely not literal. As a spirit, it's also unlikely that he would do anything that would harm a fish. What is more likely is that my uncle is telling me that he's fishing because I know that fishing made him happy when he was physically alive. So he's showing rather than telling me that he's having fun in the spirit world. These types of messages tend to comfort the grieving and convey to us that our deceased loved ones are okay. So they do serve a good purpose even if they're a bit misleading about the reality of what it's like in the afterlife.

I do believe in a review period after our physical death where we continue to learn and grow in the spirit world by reviewing our experiences in our last human lifetime. There's a lot of ground to cover when reviewing a life that's expanded 20, 30, or especially 60 or 80 years—a whole lot of choices and actions to reexamine. Even given that time doesn't exist, which is nearly impossible for us humans to fathom, that's got to take some effort and perhaps emotional energy. On the other hand, I have a story to tell you that puts all this into perspective.

I once had a reading where my father in spirit came through expressing regret and sadness for things he'd done in his life. Yet at the exact same moment, my wife, Melissa, was getting a reading with a different medium where my father came through expressing joy, love, and excitement regarding his human life.

Since both mediums gave us compelling evidence that they were in fact communicating with my father, what this shows me is that my father was able to choose his point of reference depending upon the situation (in this case, depending upon whom he was communicating with—Melissa or me). With Melissa, he was referencing experiences about his life that made him joyful, and with me, he was referencing experiences in his life that made him regretful—in order to convey different messages to each of us.

We can learn a lot from these simultaneous readings that Melissa and I experienced. For instance, one might have quickly interpreted my reading by saying that my father was still in a transitionary period in the afterlife because he was feeling regret for things he'd done that had negatively affected me. But when considering the two readings together, it leads one to believe that my father is learning and growing from *all* the events of his life concurrently. He's neither in a regretful and sad transition nor a joyful and excited transition; he's simply experiencing it all at the same time—no transitionary period necessary.

Our true nature as spirits is light. We are pure energy. Although we are clearly recognizable to one another in the afterlife (by energetic vibration), we have no bodies. We don't even have faces. We communicate by thought. To travel somewhere, we merely need to think of the place or the person we want to visit, and like magic, we are there. Consequently, as beings of light, we have no need for food, shelter, clothing, or sleep. But we get to create whatever reality we wish, if we have any desire for it.

So why do people in spirit communicate through mediums that they are still fishing, playing bridge, or painting in the afterlife? Because they are conveying a message to their loved ones through that medium that they are okay and they are happy. And because we remember our loved ones being happy when they were doing these activities, those messages ease our minds by conveying that they are in a joyful, peaceful place in the afterlife. The message is more of a metaphor than an exact description because it's incredibly difficult to explain to us what they're really doing in the spirit world (especially during a brief reading). Given the fact that mediumship is a challenging means of communication (although the best we have), communicating in metaphors is the easiest way for them to tell us they're enjoying being back home in the spirit world.

—⟋⟍—

What do we do in the spirit world?

There is no singular answer to this question. You'd have to ask individual people in spirit what they do in the afterlife for a definitive answer, and then it would only be about that individual's private experience. But there are some common things that people in spirit have mentioned (through mediums) to give you an idea of the possibilities.

When you die and cross over to the other side, you'll initially meet with loved ones in spirit who are there to greet you and welcome you home. It's basically like having a welcome-home party. Then you'll process the life that you just lived with the assistance of advanced spiritual beings. This is called a life review, and this is where you'll take away the lessons and growth that you gained from your physical life.

While all this is happening, you'll also catch up on what's happening with your surviving loved ones back on the physical plane. You'll be fully aware of all that's going on with them, especially their grief for your loss. You likely attend your own funeral services, and you might try sending them a signal that you still exist, what is called an after-death communication.

After-death communications might include you filling their room with a fragrance that reminds them of you, perhaps the smell of your cologne or the scent of cigars, banana bread, or your favorite flower (whatever might make them think of you). Other forms of after-death communication include lights flickering, candles blowing out, birds or other animals looking into their window, or perhaps even showing up in your loved ones' dreams.

Once you've become reacquainted with the spirit world again, you are likely to want to visit with loved ones in spirit whom you haven't seen in some time. This might be a family member, a friend, or even a soul you know from another lifetime.

Or you might choose to attend classes to learn about fear, forgiveness, or emotions that are more generally associated with physical incarnation (human life). As odd as it might seem, many people in spirit have communicated this idea that schools exist in the afterlife. But spirits aren't learning reading, writing, and arithmetic; the classes in the spirit world have more to do with lessons that assist with our spiritual growth. For example, I learned during a life-between-lives regression that my soul teaches about fear. Since we don't feel fear in the spiritual dimension, it's something that many people in spirit are interested in understanding, especially if they haven't yet experienced a human life.

We also have the equivalent of jobs in the spirit world, although we don't work for money as we don't need money in spirit. Some people in spirit help the newly crossed over, while others help with specific circumstances, such as sudden deaths, suicides, mass murders, or child deaths. There are even people who work with the spirits of animals that cross over. Although these are sometimes referred to as jobs, they are more like callings that provide us with fulfillment, understanding, and spiritual growth.

How we spend our time (for lack of a better word since time doesn't exist in the afterlife) has infinite options. We might choose to serve as someone's spirit guide. We might act as a counselor, helping people in spirit process their last life. We might even coordinate coincidences for people on the physical plane to help guide them toward the experiences they preplanned for their life. The possibilities are almost as endless as the spirit world itself, which means there is one thing that doesn't exist in the afterlife—boredom.

—☓—

If there is an afterlife, does that mean there's a hell?

I have seen no evidence of hell in my investigations of the afterlife. I've had hundreds of personal readings with mediums and witnessed hundreds of other people get readings, and never have I heard a single person in spirit say that they were in hell or that they were aware of such a place. I've also never heard any of them say they knew someone who was in hell or that a deceased person was missing from the spirit world (who might be in hell).

More and more afterlife experts agree that the only hell that exists is within our own physical mind. It's not a place, realm, or dimension; it's a state of human mental anguish. Fear is hell. Guilt is hell. Regret is hell. Shame is hell. And these are emotions that we can feel in the afterlife too, but only in response to our lives here on the earth plane. In this way, it's easy to understand why one might interpret the existence of hell. But this is a far stretch from a place of eternal damnation, fire, and torture.

While 10 percent to 15 percent of people who have had near-death experiences have suggested they experienced some version of what might be interpreted as hell, the evidence of near-death experiences indicates two important factors: (1) that the details of what we experience in the NDE are interpreted by our own points of reference (what we believe as human beings) and (2) that the initial experiences we have of the afterlife during the NDE are in direct relation to our expectations of it.

So if you remember that we can be, do, and have anything we want in spirit, then you understand how easily we might create a hell-like experience when we cross over to the other side during the NDE, especially if that's what we are expecting. Our beliefs alone might make it so. Still, the hell these people experienced is not what most people think of as hell (a place of eternal damnation). Instead, it is a hell-like environment of their own creation, which they can change at any moment simply by changing their thoughts (although most people who have this experience don't know they can do this).

If you've ever been to a hypnosis demonstration, you've probably witnessed volunteers from the audience being influenced by suggestion onstage. In almost every show, the hypnotist will put something like a penny in the volunteers' hands and suggest that it's getting hotter and hotter. Eventually, all the volunteers onstage drop the penny as if it's melting the palms of their hands. Yet it isn't. There is no reality to their experience of being burned by the penny. No hypnotist could afford the lawsuits if their hands were actually burned. Instead, the people experienced what they expected to experience due to the hypnotic suggestion, which was to feel the penny getting hot.

If we've learned anything from near-death experiences, it is that we can create our own reality in the spiritual dimension. One near-death experiencer told me that when she thought of a field—shazam!—she was in a field. When she then changed her thought from a field to a tunnel—shazam!—she was in a tunnel. When she then changed her thought to being in the hospital with her physical body—shazam!—she was walking down a hallway in the hospital. She said everything felt so real to her that she could feel the warmth of the sun in the field, smell the dirt of the dank tunnel, and hear the echo inside the concrete walls of the hospital. But the point is that all she needed to do was change her thought, and it changed her environment.

Consequently, my investigation has led me to conclude that people who experienced hellish near-death experiences did so because they believed in hell and that they would go there when they died. In fact, there are people whose near-death experience began as if they were in hell until they realized that they could change their environment by changing their thoughts (or calling out for help, which is another way of thinking about a new possibility). Then their hell-like environment instantly changed to a heaven-like environment.

People in spirit who communicate through mediums also say there's no hell. Channelers who channel advanced spirits and group entities agree. Even the majority of people who have had near-death experiences say there's no hell. But for those few who experienced hellish near-death experiences, the most practical explanation for their accounts is that their mind was so filled with an expectation that hell exists (and that they would go there) that hell is what they experienced. Little did they know that all they had to do was think of a more pleasant experience, or even call out for help, and their negative experience would have been over in an instant.

If you believe in hell and expect that you're going there, it's likely that you might experience what you expect, at least briefly. This doesn't mean that hell exists. What it means is that we can be, do, and have anything we can imagine in the spirit world. So if you are expecting a reality that is your imagined version of hell, that might be what you experience, at least on your way to the spirit world. Once in the spirit world—with no chance of returning to your body—there will be people in spirit there to help you end the hellish experience of your imagined expectations and see the reality of the afterlife, which is just the opposite of what we think of as hell.

This, however, brings me back to what I said about emotions like fear, guilt, regret, and shame. It doesn't matter if you're in the afterlife or you're in your physical life right now. If you're feeling fearful, guilty, regretful, or shameful about something, you're already experiencing a kind of hell. So if you die feeling those feelings, the mental hell that you were experiencing in this life is going to follow you into the afterlife. By this, I mean you will always remember what you experienced in this life—be it good or bad.

So if you currently feel remorse about something you did to someone in this lifetime, you're going to feel that remorse in the spirit world too. Once we're in spirit, we know exactly how badly we've hurt people, and we can feel what we did to them from their perspective. That's a heavy burden to carry, but it's how we learn compassion as spiritual beings. Even though we might not learn it while we're alive as humans, we can't escape it once we've crossed over to the other side.

Luckily, as mentioned, there are people in spirit who have made it their job to help the recently deceased deal with these sorts of negative emotions. Any one of us might need the gentle care and counseling of nonjudgmental spirits to help us overcome our own judgments against things we've said and done to others. This is how we process our physical lives and how we evolve spiritually from them. Eventually, we all learn to forgive ourselves for hurting or taking advantage of others, and our negative emotions turn into positive emotions. So even if you choose to call this experience of emotional transformation hell, it's temporary and beneficial—all part of our spiritual growth.

Most people who have had near-death experiences, as well as many mediums who have communicated with thousands of spirits, will go one step further and say that no one is punished in the spirit world. At best, we're tougher on ourselves than anyone in spirit will ever be on us.

As I wrote at the beginning of this book, life is about experiences. Therefore, we learn and grow even from the mistakes we've made. When you consider that we, as souls, have lived many lives—possibly thousands or more—one poor choice or act during one lifetime is but a blip in relation to all the choices and actions over all your lifetimes. Even a whole lifetime of poor choices does not damn a soul to eternal anguish. While that soul will contemplate those actions to understand them, the next life (or lives) will likely balance that karma by being on the other side of such actions in order to gain compassion for that side of the experience. Just to be clear, karma is not about punishment; it's about knowing both sides of an experience in order to gain the deepest understanding and compassion in reference to it.

—⁊⁊⁊—

Are we judged or punished for our wrongdoings when we arrive in the afterlife?

If you missed it, you should start with my answer above about hell. Beyond that, the short answer is no; we are not judged or punished for our wrongdoings in the way most people expect. However, there is also no escaping the things we did or said that brought pain, fear, harm, or suffering to another.

As mentioned, one of the events we experience upon our arrival back home in the spirit world is known as a life review. In the life review, we revisit our entire life from beginning to end, taking special notice of the significant events that hold important lessons for us.

For example, the life review will remind us of all the wonderful deeds we did to help other people. If we helped an elderly woman cross the road, we might revisit that. If we volunteered at a homeless shelter, we might revisit that too. If we smiled at a stranger one day, that also might be an act we review. And if we prayed for the sake of others or gave a kidney to save another person's life, we would most definitely review those acts as well.

The life review process gives us omniscient observation to know what the people we've affected were thinking and feeling when we interacted with them. We might feel the sense of security felt by the elderly woman as we walked across the road together as well as the gratitude in her heart. We might see how our work at the shelter affected a homeless girl by helping her to not have to steal in order to eat and find shelter. And our simple smile at the stranger might have stopped that person from completing suicide because he felt a connection with another person that he hadn't felt in weeks.

At the other end of this life review process, we also observe how our choices, words, and actions negatively affected others. If we teased and tormented a small boy in school, we will know firsthand how that affected him during that time and throughout his lifetime. We will feel his emotions and any physical pain we caused him. If we shot a deer during a hunting trip, we will know the pain we inflicted upon it and feel the fear in that animal as we hunted it and it awaited death. And if we took our frustrations out on a taxi driver one morning, we will know how our words affected his day (and possibly his life) and feel the emotions our choices ignited within him.

The life review will also show us the ripple effect of our choices, words, and actions. If the boy we teased grew up to hurt others, we will know the experiences of those people too, with the understanding that we played a part in it. If the taxi driver spread negativity to all his customers that day following his hurtful interaction with us, we will see how this affected those people and then how those people affected others and so on until the ripples end.

This works in the positive too. So if the person whose life was saved by our donated kidney lives on to positively affect the lives of others, we will know these effects with a deep understanding of whatever part we played in it.

There are no spiritual beings sitting in judgment during our life review. Because we are beings of love, we are hard enough on ourselves when we are reminded how we hurt another, whether physically or emotionally. However, there are people in spirit who have taken on the job of helping us. They help us to understand and learn from our misdeeds, and they teach us how to forgive ourselves and grow from these errors. And since we also have our good deeds and positive acts from which to balance our self-judgment, these spiritual beings remind us of them to heal our shame and regret.

I experienced a life review during what's called a life-between-lives regression (also known as a spiritual regression). This type of regression begins with a past life and then continues after your death in that lifetime as you travel in the spirit world—the life between lives. In this regression, I remembered an experience I had in the spirit world following a human lifetime in the 1600s. I experienced this life review in the presence of spiritual guides called the Council of Elders. I'll never forget the unconditional love, forgiveness, and compassion I felt from these spiritual beings. The experience was immensely powerful.

I remember how much these spirit guides (the elders) comforted me as I went through my life review process and felt horrendous regret and self-loathing for mistakes I made in that lifetime. But I was the only being judging my past behaviors. And while my own judgment was pretty severe punishment in itself, these elders helped me turn my self-judgment around so that I learned from my mistakes and grew from them. This regression experience was compelling evidence that allowed me to know on a spiritual level that we are not judged for our wrongdoings.

—◊◊—

How do our religious beliefs and practices affect us in the afterlife?

With so many religions teaching conflicting dogma, it's impossible for all religions to be correct. So the real question within this question is, what happens to people in the afterlife if their religious beliefs are wrong?

On the surface, nothing happens except that you might be surprised when you get there that your beliefs about the spirit world were so mistaken. But it will require very little to overcome your erroneous beliefs, just a little more than a quick shake of your ethereal head.

Since you were fully aware of the realities of the spirit world before you were born into this life, it's not like this is new information to you. You merely need to become reacquainted with it. It's as simple as reconnecting with a forgotten memory, which is easy to do now that your human brain no longer affects you.

So the next question that arises in regard to this is, will people whose religious beliefs are incorrect in any way be punished or banished in the afterlife? And the answer is no, of course not. Our conscious memories of the spirit world and our spiritual essence have been erased for a reason. This is part of the challenge of being human, getting through life without a manual on how to do it and what to believe. We're certainly not punished for coming to the wrong conclusions or trusting in the wrong spiritual beliefs. That would be like setting ourselves up for failure, and that's not the point of having a human life.

It's important to remember that we chose to be here. As spiritual beings (nonphysical beings), we made the choice to experience a human life. We certainly wouldn't set ourselves up for failure knowing we might be punished when we return if we didn't choose the right religion to follow, if there were such a thing.

All evidence indicates that we preplan our lives before we are born, so we already know what our religion is likely going to be before we enter this life. Just like we know who our parents, siblings, and friends are going to be, we know what religion we'll learn from our family or community as children. Our own free will allows us to choose our religion as we grow into adulthood, but it is our childhood religion that helps set the stage for how we think and act, which in turn affects who we are as people. And this is all part of our human journey. In other words, there is no right or wrong in terms of our human religion once we've crossed over to the spirit world. It's just part of our experience here on the physical plane.

—w—

What happens to atheists in the afterlife?

The same thing that happens to everyone in the afterlife happens to atheists. Just like people whose religious beliefs are erroneous (by promoting judgment, hatred, and/or separation, for instance), atheists arrive in the afterlife with great surprise. The moment they see their deceased loved ones in spirit greeting them home, they realize they had it wrong.

Even those atheists who had hoped death was the end for one reason or another (maybe because they didn't want to have to face some of the things they did or said in this lifetime) will arrive in the hereafter pleased that they were wrong. Once we cross over and feel the immense love, peace, and joy of the spiritual world, even atheists are happy to discover the error of their beliefs.

—w—

Which religion is closest to the truth?

There's no direct answer to this question. The better question would be, what part of each religion is closest to the truth? What I can tell you is that every religion that promotes love over all else has got that part right, which includes peace, forgiveness, and compassion. And those that promote fear, judgment, separation, or hate have veered off course.

In all my work with mediums and channelers, I've never had a person in spirit tell me that there is one best or most accurate religion. What spirits indicate as important is that we love one another equally, unconditionally, and unselfishly, we forgive ourselves and other people for all wrongdoings (this might be the most difficult one), and we treat everyone with the same respect and dignity that we would give our creator (Source, Universe, God).

This doesn't mean we should allow others to abuse, hurt, or take advantage of us. Nor does it mean we don't protect ourselves and don't put people who are a danger to society in prison. None of this is about being a pushover, wimp, or doormat. It's about being loving in our thoughts, words, and actions to every human being on earth.

When deciding how to act and whose example to follow, the more accurate question to ask ourselves is, what would I do in this situation if I were acting out of pure love and in the best interest of everyone affected by my choice? Your answer to that question will lead you in the right direction every time.

—ɷ—

Is death permanent, or do we have more than one life?

My experiences have shown me that we as spiritual beings live many, many human lives. Although the evidence is clear from mediums' communications with spirits and from what near-death experiencers have learned while in the spirit world, the strongest evidence that we live more than one life comes from past-life regression.

In case you missed what I've mentioned on this subject earlier, a past-life regression is when a person is led into their subconscious memories of a previous lifetime by a hypnotic regressionist using guided meditation. The fact that millions of people all over the world have had this experience is strong evidence that past lives exist. And if past lives exist, then that means we live more than one life.

My own past-life regressions have taught me that we most certainly live more than one life. When I experienced these past lives—which is a multisensory experience where I could see, smell, taste, feel, and hear things—each regression brought me beyond belief into a "knowing" that we live multiple lives. And as I reexperienced each lifetime in my regression memories, it felt like remembering something long forgotten. The experience was so real and had such depth that there was absolutely no question that I had lived these lives as these different people. As a result, these experiences alone taught me that we (as souls) live multiple lifetimes. My experiences with mediums and near-death experiencers simply added to this evidence.

—⚬⚬—

Can my loved one see or hear me from the spirit world?

Oh yes, all our loved ones can both see *and* hear us from the afterlife. Even better, they can read our thoughts telepathically, which means that we don't have to talk out loud to them in order for them to hear us.

Having said this, my father in spirit has suggested through mediums that he prefers when I talk out loud to him. He likes when I talk to him as if he were right in the room with me because, of course, he is. Even though I can't see or hear him, he can see and hear me just fine. He simply isn't vibrating at a frequency that my eyes and ears can perceive him, sort of in the same way that I can't hear a dog whistle, but dogs can. And since my father is in my presence, he prefers that I communicate to him as I did when he was with me in physical form. Many people in spirit have communicated through mediums that they feel the same way.

So go ahead, and talk out loud to your loved ones in spirit. I suggest doing this in private because other people might not understand. But talk out loud to your deceased loved ones knowing that they are in the room with you and communicating back to you telepathically. Pay attention to the thoughts that are popping into your mind (in the form of words, pictures, or feelings) because it could be your loved one communicating back to you.

A friend of mine lost her husband a couple years ago and was out for a walk while talking to him in her mind. Every time she said something to him, she felt like she heard him in her mind talking back in response. Still slightly skeptical because the voice she heard in her head was her own, she asked him to give her a sign that would help her to know it was really him talking back to her. The next thing she heard in her head was "Your mother wants a new blue dress."

A couple of days later, my friend saw her mother and asked her if she had been thinking about getting a new dress. Her mother responded, "Oh yes, I've been looking at a beautiful blue dress in a store. I keep going back to look at it, but I can't get myself to spend the money."

—⁓—

Are our deceased loved ones watching over us from the spirit world?

Yes, our deceased loved ones do watch over us from the spirit world. It's a tricky phenomenon to explain because, once again, there is no time or distance in the spiritual realm. But suffice it to say that our loved ones know everything we are doing.

Does that mean they are following us around everywhere? No, not exactly. They don't need to stalk us. Since time and distance don't exist where they are, they merely need to check in on us to see what we've been doing. Think of it like they have a DVR (like TiVo), and all they have to do is check the Recorded menu to watch our most recent events. In reality, it's even better than a DVR because all they have to do is think of us to instantly download all our most recent happenings, more like movies on demand.

It's very common in a reading with a medium that the sitter's loved ones in spirit convey to the medium what the sitter has been up to recently—what they've been doing, saying, and even thinking. These are events that the psychic medium in most cases could never know. The spirit might mention that she saw her husband visiting her gravesite, was present during his birthday party, and is aware of his recent promotion. And the specifics of what they witnessed during such events can be quite detailed, such as knowing that he brought a bottle of champagne to the cemetery in order to toast their wedding anniversary. These types of messages from a medium are strong evidence to show that our loved ones in spirit are with us and are aware of what's going on in our lives.

But you needn't worry that our loved ones in spirit are focusing too much on our lives and not enough on their own spiritual lives. Nonphysical beings are able to do more than one thing at a time, which leads to the next question.

—‍ɷ‍—

How can my loved one in spirit watch over my sister and me at the same time?

There's a fantastic documentary on near-death experiences (NDEs) by Dr. Raymond Moody titled *Life after Life.* In this movie, a woman talks about her NDE, saying that (and I'm paraphrasing) while she watched her body lying dead in the operating room of the hospital and heard everything the doctors were saying while trying to revive her, she was simultaneously able see and hear her brother-in-law in the hallway talking on the phone, while at the same time see her sister in a different state of the country searching for her keys in order to go to the store, while at the same time be outside the hospital, where she could see a red sneaker sitting on the windowsill of one of the hospital rooms located several stories above the ground.

Later, after the woman was resuscitated and she recovered from her temporary death, everything this woman heard and saw was verified as true—right up to what the doctors said in the operating room and what her brother-in-law said on the telephone. It's a fascinating yet typical account of what is possible when we leave our physical bodies and enter the spiritual state. And it's evidence that spirits can be in several places at the same time.

People in spirit are not limited by distance or time, so your loved ones are fully able to be with you in the United States and your sibling in England at the exact same moment. And this is true no matter how many people are involved. As I indicated earlier when answering the question about what spirits wear and eat in the spirit world, my wife, Melissa, and I each had separate readings one day at the exact same time, but with different mediums, and my father came through in both our readings. This was early in my investigation of the afterlife, so you can imagine my surprise. But I was glad it happened because it taught me early in my investigation of the afterlife that spirits are not limited by time and distance.

—⟆⟆—

My father died before I had my baby. Is Dad aware of his grandson?

If your father died before your baby was born, then your father knew your son before you did. So your son got to meet his grandfather because they were in the spirit world together before your son was ever born.

It's helpful to keep in mind that we're referring to your father's soul and your son's soul, so we're not really talking about an old man and a baby. Instead, we're referring to two souls who knew of their human roles as grandfather and grandson. Nonetheless, they knew each other in the spirit world before your son was born.

In this same line of thought, you, your father, and your son all knew one another in the spirit world before any of you were born because we plan our lives before we are born. Many spirits (through psychic mediums) and spirit masters (through channelers) have indicated that we chart our lives before arriving here, and that includes all the other souls who will share that lifetime with us—parents, relatives, friends, teachers, bosses, and more.

I had what's called a life-between-lives regression (also known as a spiritual regression), where I experienced a past life and then continued the regression beyond my death in that lifetime to the spirit world. What I experienced in this life-between-lives regression was a knowing that I shared many lives with a group of souls (my soul group), although we all changed relationships (as well as genders) from lifetime to lifetime.

Your father is also fully aware of your child simply because he's aware of everything in your life. Spirits often say in readings of spirit communication that they are closer to us in spirit than they could ever be in the physical world. All this means is that spirits know more about our lives, our thoughts, and our feelings than is *humanly* possible, mostly because humans don't read minds and feel emotions telepathically as effectively as spirits.

Using this example, your father in spirit would know your child better than he could have ever known him if he were still humanly alive simply because he has the advantage of knowing your child from a spirit observer point of view. This means he has the ability to know your son's thoughts and feelings, such as his joys and sorrows, better than he could ever understand these things while on the physical plane.

One of the wonderful benefits of understanding the afterlife due to my investigations is that I no longer worry that my loved ones might miss something in my future if they die early. Since I know the afterlife exists and I know my loved ones are watching over me, I also know they won't miss anything that happens in my life after they've passed.

My father died before my first book was ever published, but I know that he is fully aware of that accomplishment in my life. In fact, he actually told me he was proud of that achievement during a reading I had with a medium who was a complete stranger to me, meaning she had no idea that I was a published author. This sort of thing has happened in many of my readings with mediums. I've also witnessed this while watching hundreds of other people's readings. So live your life knowing that your loved ones in spirit don't miss any of your accomplishments, be that a wedding, birth, graduation, anniversary, birthday, award, honor, or any other event you might celebrate during your life.

—◊—

Who will greet me in the spirit world when I die?

All your deceased loved ones will greet you when you die, especially those you love and trust the most. For one, they want you to know you are safe. They don't want you to feel any fear while your conscious mind shifts back from physical life to spiritual knowing.

But fear is of no real concern since feeling safe happens inevitably because the light of the afterlife blankets you with the most intense feelings of security, love, warmth, and joy. As you transition from the physical back to the spiritual—which all happens very naturally and automatically (with no effort on your part)—the closer you progress to the light, the more powerful these feelings will get.

According to people in spirit who have communicated with mediums, your closest relationships from this lifetime will be waiting for you first. If this is a parent, grandparent, sibling, spouse, or best friend, they will be there. There is no single protocol, so you might initially see just one loved one and the others will follow (most common), or you might be greeted by two or five people in spirit with many others to follow.

Many people in spirit, as well as those who have had near-death experiences, have described being greeted by loved ones in spirit initially yet also *knowing* that others were waiting their turn to say hello just behind them. Some who have had near-death experiences have explained that they could feel the strong energy of these spirits in the background like a wave of love encircling them.

Your pets in the spirit world will also greet you. They too are anxious to see you again. And this is true for any animal you have loved: cats, dogs, horses, goats, bunnies, hamsters, and birds.

You'll also be greeted by any person who has played a significant and loving role in your life, be it a teacher, mentor, or boss. Schoolmates and coworkers might also arrive to your homecoming celebration, waiting, of course, until you have seen your closest loved ones first. Basically, everyone you've loved who died before you is excited to reunite with you again, so there is no one who you want to see who won't be there.

On the other hand, this is your celebration, so you don't need to worry that anyone whom you don't want to see will arrive. Your wishes are respected and honored here. You don't even have to tell anyone your wishes because everyone can read your thoughts. Plus they already know who you don't want at your party because they know you better than you can imagine—they've been reading your thoughts your entire life.

Your spirit guides (those spirits who guided you throughout your life) will also be there to greet you. Although you might not realize it now, you and your guides have a very special relationship. Before you left the spirit world to be born, you personally chose your guides, trusting them to take the utmost care of you from the spiritual realm. So your spirit guides are like dear friends who you literally trust with your life. And because you knew them before you were born, you will recognize them at your reunion.

—⚹—

Which husband will greet me when I cross over if I've had more than one husband?

If you've had more than one husband and provided they're both in the spirit world, the one you feel closest with will likely be the first to greet you. But if you feel equally comfortable with both, then they might both come to see you at the same time. We must keep in mind that there is no jealousy or competitiveness on the spiritual plane. As spirits, your first and second husbands—as well as your third, fourth, and fifth, if that were the case—would all feel a kinship together because of their love for you. Jealousy and competitiveness are human emotions and are not felt by spirits. Each husband would know his importance in your life and the spiritual growth for which he was significant, which spirits know are not reduced by the importance and significance of another.

There are no hard and fast rules here, but spirits who have communicated through mediums and people who have had near-death experiences have all indicated that our transition back home to the spirit world is designed to make us feel safe and joyful. So if you don't want to see one husband because of some bad energy between you on the physical plane, that husband is not going to burden you with his presence upon your return home. Later, after you have settled back into your spiritual existence (and only when you are ready), you and that former husband can work on healing those negative memories. But it won't happen until it's something that you want and choose to do.

—⟋⟋—

Will I always be with my loved ones in the afterlife?

Life in the spirit world isn't all that different than life here in the physical world in terms of being with our loved ones. The most wonderful part about spirit life is that all we have to do is ask in our minds to be with someone, and we are with them. We don't have to walk, drive, or fly to visit someone. So in this way, you will always be with the people you love in the afterlife.

Just like in our human lives, people in spirit aren't constantly side by side. Because we as spirits are pure energy, each one of us vibrates at a different frequency, which determines where in the spiritual dimension we exist. Some people like to call these different locations "levels." More accurately, they are levels of vibration.

We increase our vibration through spiritual growth, which has nothing to do with religion as there is no religion in the afterlife. The kinder, gentler, more peaceful, more forgiving, more compassionate, and more loving we are, the higher our vibration. This is one of the benefits of experiencing a physical life as a human being. Our growth as humans speeds up our vibration, which benefits us as spiritual beings. Even when we act selfishly, competitively, and negatively as humans, our souls learn and evolve from that lower-vibration experience. It's not that we'll be proud of it when back in spirit, but we'll recognize the error of our ways and will grow from having the experience.

In terms of traveling around the spirit world, psychic mediums, channelers, and people who have had life-between-lives regressions say we can only go to levels that match our vibrational frequency or lower. So people in spirit that you know who are vibrating at a higher frequency must come down to your level because you can't go to theirs. Think of this more as a law of physics than a rule. This is the same reason why humans can't visit the spirit world for the weekend (because we vibrate at a lower frequency), yet spirits can visit us here on the physical plane anytime they please. These same principles hold true in the spirit world. Having said that, anytime a spirit wants to meet with a loved one who is at a higher level, all we need to do is think of them (with the intention of wanting to visit them), and they will appear.

Most people don't realize it, but life on the physical plane shares many similarities with life in spirit. You've probably noticed that you tend to hang around with people who are similar to you during various stages of your life. This is because you and your friends, for instance, are all vibrating at a similar frequency. You've probably heard the saying "Like attracts like." We gravitate toward one another because we're vibrating at a similar frequency, which usually coincides with the fact that we have a lot in common.

You'll notice that no matter where you go—the mall, the movie theater, or the hairdressing salon—you tend to run into the same people. Yet whenever you make a shift in consciousness and become more loving and compassionate as a result, one day, you recognize that you're no longer running into those people anymore. Suddenly, you've made new friends or have at least recognized that you have less in common with your old friends, even if you're hanging on to those relationships out of loyalty, complacency, or fear of change. Nonetheless, one day, when you go to the mall, movie theater, or hair salon, you realize you're running into new friends. And at some point, you rarely ever see your old friends anymore—because you're vibrating at different frequencies—so you're not even on the same vibrational level anymore. It's as if you live in different worlds. And the truth is that, vibrationally, you do.

It's impossible to describe in human terms what it's really like in the spirit world, but the answer is yes, you do get to be with your loved ones there if you so desire.

—⁓—

Will I still be married to my spouse in the afterlife?

The answer is both yes and no. The answer is yes because the memories of every life we live become an eternal part of our soul's journey. And every life and every relationship is sacred and meaningful. So this will be true for you and your spouse. It is a relationship that will stay with you both forever in memory. And memory in spirit has a much deeper meaning than memory to us as humans.

The answer is also no because marriage is a human concept, so it doesn't really fit into the reality of the spirit world. However, we are able to continue with those roles during our shift back into the afterlife until we are ready to embrace our spiritual essence. In actuality, though, we don't need to maintain our human roles. Relationships are much richer and more intimate in spirit than we can possibly imagine as humans. There are no hidden secrets between spirits since we can read one another's minds. Therefore, there is no need for best-friend pacts or marriage contracts. Relationships are completely organic and authentic.

While relationships carried over from our physical lives always remain special to us, once we cross over and recognize the intense connections we have in the spirit world, we no longer crave the human marriage relationship that we knew from our human life. And of course, since we are beings of light (pure energy), sexual relations no longer exist either.

Still, my answer to this question is not meant to minimize the significance of our human relationships. Loving relationships like the spousal relationship are bonds that last for all eternity. The intimacy and affection shared between souls is never forgotten. We are not just playing roles here on the physical plane like actors in a theatrical production. What we do as human beings matters. Human relationships are much more challenging than relationships in spirit, so there's immense pride in spirit when we've made a human relationship work. Our words, our actions, and even our thoughts hold considerable meaning and consequence. Thus, you and your spouse will carry the significance of your relationship with you to the other side.

I have been with my wife, Melissa, since she was 12, and I was 15 years old. We were childhood sweethearts who rarely left one another's side. For most of our lives, we have spent every single day together. We live together, work together, and play together. It's a very special bond.

As nice as that is, I won't be surprised to learn that my wife, Melissa, is more spiritually advanced than me, which means that she vibrates at a higher frequency. I've never met another person who is so loving, unselfish, and compassionate toward people, animals, and even insects. She is my greatest teacher in this life by example alone, and I am a better human being due to her insightful advice and words of wisdom.

As a result, let's suppose that Melissa will reside at a higher level than me in the spirit world. It's important she be surrounded by people in spirit who are at her level (in frequency and wisdom) in order for her to continue to learn and grow. But that doesn't sadden me because I know our bond will last forever. We'll always remember this special love we've shared during this lifetime. That doesn't mean we need to spend every moment of eternity side by side. Yet at the same time, I have no doubt that we'll share other physical lifetimes together. We might be siblings, friends, or even rivals, but I welcome any additional human life that I can spend in her presence.

Do we continue our spiritual growth in the spirit world?

We most certainly continue our spiritual growth in the spirit world. Spirits often talk about it when conveying messages through mediums.

Channelers speak of it. And it was evident in my own life-between-lives regressions.

In the spiritual realm, we grow by going to school. We grow by teaching others. We grow by guiding spirits having a human life. We grow by assisting people who are crossing back over into the spirit world after having a human life. The opportunities for growth in the spiritual dimension are endless.

This question is actually kind of funny if you think it through. Asking if we continue our spiritual growth in the spirit world is a lot like asking if we continue to make money at our place of employment or if we continue to get fit at the gym. Since the spirit world is our true home and our true essence is that of spirit, it makes sense that we would continue to grow spiritually after we return home to the afterlife.

Our life here on earth (the physical plane) is a temporary trip we make from the spirit world. Therefore, the more logical question would be to ask if we continue our spiritual growth here on the earth plane, and that answer would be yes as well. Apparently, a human life is a lot like boot camp, where we learn and grow a lot in a short amount of time.

Experiencing a human life is only one of many opportunities for spiritual growth. There are other dimensions, places of existence, and even living forms that our souls choose to experience. And there's a lot to learn in the afterlife itself. Just like we (as physical beings) learn and grow from watching the lives of other people here on earth, people in spirit get to observe other people living on the physical plane (or in other dimensions and places) and see what they are doing well or what they could be doing better. Likewise, we get to talk with people in spirit who have had many lives and learn what lessons they have to teach us. Even when we ourselves teach other people in spirit the lessons we've learned from our various lifetimes, we grow to master those lessons even more by teaching them.

Keep in mind that the spirit world grants us access to anyone we'd like to meet. Since people in spirit can be in multiple places at one time, even those who were famous on the physical plane are willing and able to talk with us. Imagine being able to ask questions of anyone in history: Winston Churchill, Martin Luther King Jr., Napoleon Hill, Mother Teresa, Henry Ford, Leonardo da Vinci, William Shakespeare, Anne Frank, Gandhi, Socrates, Abraham Lincoln, John Lennon, or Babe Ruth. Consider the wisdom you'd learn from their successes and mistakes. What a treasure trove of information they'd be.

Ironically, once we have returned to the afterlife and now have this unlimited access to people of notoriety in spirit, we as spirits don't yearn to meet them just because they're famous. The thrill of meeting celebrities is another human characteristic that doesn't carry over to spirits. After all, we've likely all been famous in one lifetime or another. And there's no fame in the spiritual dimension. So even though we have greater access to people like those mentioned above, it's unlikely that we as spirits will care to connect with them unless we're trying to learn about something that they experienced or happen to teach.

PART FOUR

—ɷ—

QUESTIONS ABOUT SPIRITS, ANGELS, AND GHOSTS

What's the difference between a spirit, a ghost, and an angel?

The word 'spirit' is just another way of describing a person who is in "spiritual form" versus "physical form." Said another way, a spirit is a person who is a spiritual being as opposed to a human being.

You and I are spiritual beings having a physical (human) experience— that is, spirits inhabiting a physical (human) body. We are spirits by nature, so our spiritual essence is eternal, while our physical human bodies are temporary. When our spirit leaves our body, our bodies cease to survive, but our consciousness continues.

When we refer to spirits in reference to a medium reading (a reading of spirit communication), we are generally referring to the spirit of a deceased loved one. So when a medium says that your mother's spirit is present, he means that the consciousness and eternal essence of your mother is near. In this case, the medium can hear, see, or feel the spirit of your mother (possibly all three). For all practical purposes, the medium is communicating with your mother, except that your mother is without a physical body—she's in spirit (a spiritual being of light).

The word 'ghost' is used in so many different ways by different people that there is a lot of confusion about its meaning. Let's clear up some of these misunderstandings.

Some people use the word 'ghost' synonymously with the word 'spirit'; that is, they use both words interchangeably. As a result of my own afterlife investigation, I too consider the words 'spirit' and 'ghost' to have the same meaning. While I don't usually use the word 'ghost' at all, I see no difference between the two words.

So why do some people get scared by ghosts? It is my experience that people who are seeing ghosts are merely seeing spirits and getting scared by them because of their beliefs and expectations that ghosts are scary and possibly evil. Fearful beliefs, when strong enough, can lead folks to draw all kinds of conclusions that are not accurate.

Ghosts are not scary or evil from the evidence I've seen. They are just our loved ones in spirit trying to communicate that they still exist, they are okay, and they are watching over us. But television shows and movies are responsible for much of the fear and beliefs people have around ghosts, so I certainly understand why so many people fear them.

There are other people, however, who consider ghosts and spirits as somewhat different entities. These people believe ghosts are the spirits of people who haven't gone into the light (the light of the spirit world). Hence, many people of this belief think that ghosts are earthbound. And if you believe in haunted houses in the traditional sense that we see in movies and TV shows, it would be these earthbound ghosts who are haunting them.

The word 'angel' is as commonly misused as the word 'ghost.' Once again, many people use the word synonymously with the word 'spirit.'

In fact, more searches are done on Internet search engines for angels than spirits and ghosts together. But my research leads me to conclude that many of these searches are seeking information on spirits—they're just using the word 'angel.' There are even people who call themselves angel messengers or angel communicators who are actually working as psychic mediums. So with all these different meanings, it's no wonder so many people are confused as to the true meaning of angels.

Historically, angels are a common spiritual figure of various religions that generally serve as a messenger or servant of God. From this point of view, most religions contend that angels are spiritually superior to spirits and, due to their angelic status, never experience a physical life. Furthermore, in their service to God, angels assist human beings by guiding and even intervening with miracles when necessary. Using this definition of angels, they also assist spirits when needed, most commonly while a person in spirit is transitioning from their human life back to spirit life.

—⚏—

What's the difference between our spirit and our soul?

Ask 10 people in this field for their definitions of the words 'spirit' and 'soul,' and you might get 10 different answers. Similar to the confusion surrounding the words 'spirit,' 'angel,' and 'ghost,' many people are confused by the words 'spirit' and 'soul' because so many people have different definitions of them. Oftentimes, these words are even used interchangeably. But from my perspective, there is a significant difference between the two words.

For the most accurate and complete answer, you should also read my explanation of spirit and soul at the beginning of this book in the section titled "Big-Picture Answers That Will Improve Your Comprehension of This Book." That section's answer is meant to work in conjunction with this answer.

From my practical viewpoint, our soul is our eternal spiritual essence that always remains in the spirit world. It is what some people call our higher self because it guides us from the spiritual realm holding the wisdom of possibly thousands of lives.

Our spirit, on the other hand, is that part of our soul that inhabits our human body in order to experience a physical life. Once it's contained within the human body, it temporarily forgets all the wisdom of the soul in order to experience a physical life with a fresh, clean slate.

The soul, however, with its immeasurable wisdom, is forever connected to the spirit. And the connection between our spirit and our soul is found through our subconscious mind, what Carl Jung called the superconscious. While our spirit journeys to the physical plane to experience a human life, the soul guides and communicates with our spirit via intuition. One challenge of every human, therefore—without knowing it—is to honor this intuitive guidance in balance with our intellect.

Since our free will gives us the final say regarding our choices in life, our spirit's subconscious connection to our soul is thus trumped by our ego, which is where the greatest human challenge ultimately lies. The ego wants to believe it is separate when, in fact, we are always connected to the soul and the Universe.

When our human body dies, our spirit leaves our body and returns to our soul, much like a raindrop evaporates from the ground and returns to the atmosphere. It is now time for the soul—at one again with our spirit—to evaluate its human life and then learn and grow from it.

So when I refer to the spirit, I'm usually referring to the spirit within the body that has voyaged to the physical dimension for a human experience. But when I refer to the soul, I'm referring to that eternal and ever-evolving spiritual being that holds the memories and wisdom of all our lives and all our experiences.

The spirit and the soul are always one, which I know can be very confusing. But think of your spirit as that part of your soul that you know as you, the individual that is living with your personality, your name, and your memories from this lifetime. And your soul, then, is every personality, every name, and every memory of every lifetime you have ever lived. So the you that you know as you is only a portion of your soul, but it is still at one with it, just as your soul is only a portion of the ultimate oneness of the Universe (with a capital U), yet your soul is still at one with It (with a capital I).

—∿—

Can a soul have more than one spirit?

Yes, each soul is able to have multiple spirits (of itself), so a soul can have multiple life experiences—even simultaneously. And when I say life experiences, I mean all sorts of living experiences in many various life forms, including life forms on other planets, in other galaxies, and even within other dimensions of which we are not aware.

There is no compelling evidence of a soul experiencing more than one human life at the same time, but that doesn't mean it isn't possible. Because each spirit that inhabits a human body has its own personality, there'd be no way to recognize two spirits from the same soul from readings with mediums, for example. But I do believe it's possible for the soul to live multiple human lives concurrently; I even believe it's probable.

This is a complicated subject, I realize, but I wanted to open your mind to these deeper possibilities. Given that we as humans view everything from the paradigm of time and space (distance), it can be challenging to wrap our minds around the idea of everything happening at the same time. But my answers about the afterlife are "drawn from" and "written for" our human paradigm, so I'm limited in accuracy right from the get-go. Nonetheless, my investigations into life after death lead me to believe our souls can have multiple spirits experiencing life in different places (and dimensions) at the same time.

—∿—

Do pets have souls?

Yes, pets (and all animals) have souls (and spirits) just like people, and they too go to the afterlife. I've been to many events where mediums gave readings to random audience members from the stage, and the medium mentioned seeing the person's deceased dog, cat, horse, guinea pig, or snake. In most cases, the medium was able to describe what the pet looked like, its personality, and characteristics about the pet that only the owner knew—all with uncanny accuracy.

It's human arrogance to think that we're the only species that gets to go to the afterlife or that we're the only species that has a spirit or a soul. It is our spirit that gives us our life energy (and our consciousness), and it is our spirit that turns our bodies from mere flesh and bones to walking, talking, thinking beings. So if there's a species on earth that has life, then there's a spirit and a soul associated with it.

Our souls have experienced life as many species and in many places, so this would include experiencing life as animals. Still, I'm not implying that "the you who you know as you" has experienced life as an animal because "the you who you know as you" is your spirit. And your spirit only experiences one life.

It is your soul—your higher self (your whole self)—that experiences many lives, which includes having experiences as other living species. So your soul has likely experienced life as an animal through a spirit that your soul created for that lifetime.

However, most people who ask if pets have souls are not wondering if they, personally, have had a life as an animal. Most people ask this question because they wonder if they will see their beloved pet in the afterlife or if they can communicate with their deceased pet now. The answer to both questions is yes. In fact, most of what you learn about humans in this book will pertain to your pets as well.

What might surprise you is that your pets will be able to communicate with you from the afterlife in spite of your animal's inability to speak our language while here on the earth plane. Since communication in the afterlife is telepathic, animals can talk to us in our dreams, during meditation, through spirit writing, and through mediums. Their thoughts convert to language in the spirit world in whatever language we speak.

So if you've lost a pet, rest assured that they are steeped in the love and light of Source Energy and are surrounded by other spirits and souls who love them. And feel free to talk to them as if they were in the room with you because they are watching over you just like all our deceased loved ones do.

There's a wonderful book by Kim Sheridan titled *Animals and the Afterlife* that covers this subject in great detail. I definitely recommend it.

—⟋⟍—

Can cats and dogs see spirits?

I can't verify with any concrete evidence that animals can see spirits, but many people believe that they can. I have certainly seen my pets staring at (and even following with their eyes) something in the room that I cannot see. It's an odd experience when you see it. And I have only witnessed this happen after losing a loved one or when talking about a loved one in spirit. While this alone certainly won't convince skeptics that animals can see spirits, it's a phenomenon that I can't explain otherwise.

—⟋⟍—

What is a spirit guide?

A spirit guide is a spirit (on the spiritual plane) who guides a spirit having a human experience (on the physical plane). In simpler words, a spirit guide is a spiritual being who is guiding a human being.

Getting much deeper in definition, a spirit guide is the spirit of a soul who has chosen to assist the spirit of another soul during the latter's human life.

I also believe that we are guided by our soul in addition to our spirit guides, which is why we often refer to our soul as our higher self.

There are many beliefs that cannot be verified regarding spirit guides, so I'll just tell you what makes the most sense to me. We each have one or more key guides (main guides) who guide us throughout our lifetime.

These are spirits who have not lived during our lifetime, so it is nobody we would know from this lifetime. Naturally, if they had lived as a human during our life, they would not have been able to guide us from above while they were here. For this reason, our principal spirit guides have always been in spirit while we've been experiencing a human life.

Many mediums have claimed that our spirit guides change as we age and grow, which seems to be accurate. However, I tend to believe that we have at least one spirit guide who sticks with us throughout our lifetime. Perhaps this one guide who always remains is simply our soul (higher self).

We also have temporary guides who do come and go throughout our lives, and this is because we have specific needs along the way. If you need help with courage, self-confidence, or a certain talent during your life, a particular spirit who specializes in that area would assist you with that matter alone. Once you no longer need that spirit's help, they move on.

Finally, some people who have had near-death experiences have indicated to me that their spirit guides were actually from their own soul, meaning their spirit and their spirit guides all originated from (and are connected to) the same soul.

This would mean that different aspects of our own soul are guiding us. I like this idea, but I have not seen a lot of evidence for it. And frankly, while I find the idea mind-blowing in a good way, it doesn't really affect us one way or the other in our human understanding of spirit guides. But I'm amused by the idea for this reason—if I don't like the way my spirit guides are guiding me, I've got no one but myself to blame for it.

—⚬—

Are my loved ones in spirit now my spirit guides?

It is possible that you have a deceased loved one who has become your spirit guide in one way or another, but it's unlikely that they are one of your main guides.

As mentioned, your main guide or guides stay with you from your birth to your death. Of course, if you have a relative who died before you were born, it's always possible that he or she is your spirit guide. That said, the human and spirit guide relationship is a sacred, special, and vitally important role that is usually given to a highly advanced spirit (after all, this is no job for an amateur). And since most highly advanced spirits no longer reincarnate, it is unlikely that they are one of your deceased loved ones.

This doesn't mean, though, that your loved ones in spirit are not watching over you and helping to guide you—they most certainly are. I have a few deceased family members who have communicated through mediums that they have assisted me with one thing or another in my life. Some are temporary projects and some are long-term endeavors. My father, for example, has shown up for all my readings with mediums (and I've tested hundreds). And I'm sure he has been assisting me with my investigation of the afterlife ever since it began in 1999.

So while your loved ones in spirit are not likely your main guides throughout your life, you probably already know which ones are helping to guide and assist you throughout your life since their passing. You might have one who helps you find missing things, like keys or eyeglasses. You might have one deceased relative who inspires your writing or artwork. Or you might have one who assists you in raising your children. The possibilities are truly endless.

—ᴍᴍ—

How can I communicate with my spirit guides?

Since our spirit guides can read our minds, we are always communicating with them because we're always thinking. But since it's common that we send out mixed messages by thinking that we want one thing and then following that with a thought that we don't deserve it or are never lucky enough to get such things, it's a smart idea to take the time to communicate directly with our spirit guides.

The easiest way to communicate with your spirit guides is to talk out loud to them as if they were right in the room with you (because, technically, they are). If you want to request something from them, tell them what you want, although follow that statement with "this or something better." It's important to say "this or something better" because it's impossible for us to consider all the possibilities that might be similar but better than what we've requested. We simply don't have the higher perspective that our guides have.

When you talk out loud to your spirit guides, tell them how you'd like your request to look or sound, how it will make you feel, and even what it will taste or smell like, if that applies. The more details you give them about your desire, the better. And I'm not just referring to material possessions here; I'm referring to every request—a request to help someone who is ill, a request for your interview to go smoothly, a request that the tornado won't hit your house, or a request that your missing cat finds his way home.

Tell your spirit guides what you're going to do to make your desire happen, and say that you'd appreciate their assistance. Too many people ask their guides for something and then just wait for them to make it happen. If all you're doing is sitting on your sofa and watching TV while waiting for a modeling agency to discover you or a publishing company to offer you a book contract, that makes it pretty difficult (though not impossible) for your spirit guides to help you. But if you actually go to modeling agencies and show them your portfolio or create a professional book proposal and submit it to publishers or agents, now you're helping your spirit guides to help you.

An alternative to simply talking out loud to your spirit guides is writing to them. You can write them a letter on your laptop, in a handwritten note, or in a journal. Write them a letter spelling out the details of your request or how you'd like your future to look. Some people are more articulate in writing, so use your talents in this endeavor. If you're a gifted artist, feel free to draw or paint your communications as well.

What's great about writing a letter is that it encourages you to add more detail about your request. You might feel silly talking out loud to your guides with no visible presence in the room, which might influence you to cut your communications short. But it's perfectly natural to write a letter, so it's more likely that you will communicate more fully than you would talking out loud. And writing is something you can do at work during your break, on the subway, or in a coffee shop.

Our spirit guides are helping us every day. The amount of assistance and guidance they provide is never-ending. So don't just ask for assistance; take the time to communicate your gratitude for everything they do for you too. Again, you can do this by talking out loud to them, thinking it, or by writing them a letter. Since we can never know everything our spirit guides do for us, all we need to do in this exercise is communicate to them how much we appreciate our blessings in life. Take one blessing a day, or list as many as you can think of in one sitting. Regardless, it's important that we communicate what we appreciate in our life so that our guides understand that we'd like more of it.

—⚞—

In what ways do my spirit guides communicate with me?

Our spirit guides are constantly guiding and communicating with us. Unfortunately, most people are not aware of it. Here are the most common ways that our spirit guides send us messages and influence us to go in the right direction.

INTUITION: First, our spirit guides communicate to us (guide us) through our *intuition*. Everyone has intuition. I'm not talking about psychic ability, although psychic ability is just enhanced intuition. Nevertheless, your intuition is nothing more than your inner sense about things, your gut feelings, your personal instincts, and those spontaneous thoughts that pop into your mind. It's important that you learn to follow these signals because much of this is guidance from your spirit guides.

COINCIDENCE: Second, our spirit guides communicate to us and guide us through *coincidence*. Some call this divine coincidence or synchronicity. Unfortunately, many people erroneously use the word 'coincidence' to mean luck, fluke, or chance, which is the kind of shortsightedness that will lead one to overlook valuable guidance from their spirit guides.

Coincidence is when two or more events occur that have no obvious relation to one another yet result in a meaningful connection or result. So if you have three totally unrelated people recommend that you see *Chicago* at the local playhouse this weekend, that's a coincidence that might be a message from your spirit guides. What's the message? Well, the possibilities are endless, but it could be that you'll meet someone there who will positively affect the rest of your life.

My wife, Melissa, crossed paths with a woman from town that she knew but rarely ever saw. In fact, she bumped into her three times in one week. When Melissa told me that she saw this woman again for the third time, I asked her what this woman represents to her—what she thinks of when she sees her. Melissa said she only knows the woman because the woman supported her friend while the friend was being treated for breast cancer. Coincidentally, Melissa had an astrology reading and I had a psychic reading that both mentioned Melissa should get checked for breast cancer. So with this final coincidence of seeing this woman three times in one week, Melissa got a checkup with her doctor. Sure enough, she was diagnosed with breast cancer at an early stage, which she subsequently treated for successfully using alternative methods. That was years ago. Melissa is now cancer-free, and we have coincidence to thank for identifying it.

MESSENGERS: Third, our spirit guides communicate with us and guide us through *messengers*. Messengers can be people, animals, or things. For example, you might be fretting over how you're going to pay a bill when a stranger on the subway tells you that she just traded in her unwanted gold jewelry for hundreds of dollars. Or you might be watching TV and see a segment on dangerous toys only to discover that your granddaughter has one of those toys in her crib. Or you might be walking your dog down the street when your dog suddenly stops, turns around, and begins walking the other way only to learn the next day that a man was robbed on that same street around that same time of day that you were walking.

This is how spirit guides communicate with us through messengers. If they can find a messenger to deliver a message or lead us in the right direction, they'll do it.

EVENTS: The fourth most common method spirit guides use to communicate with us and guide us is through *events*—things that happen to us or around us. For instance, you might get fired from your job only to land a more enjoyable job with better pay. Or your boyfriend might break up with you, which might lead to a new relationship with someone who is more loving and compatible with you. Or you might even break your ankle and begin writing that novel you've always dreamed of writing, which might become a *New York Times* best seller.

When our spirit guides communicate to us or guide us via events, it's not always going to be a seemingly negative event like getting fired or breaking an ankle. It can also be wonderful events. I met a woman who found a wallet once and ended up marrying the man who owned it. Melissa and I were given tickets to a conference once where we met a woman who became one of our closest friends—both her and her husband.

Sometimes our spirit guides guide us using two or more methods of communication and guidance. I have a friend who was given tickets to a concert, and while driving to the concert hall, he got into a fender bender with another car. Following the minor accident, his car was towed to a body shop because the fender prevented the front wheels from turning. Once his car was in the body shop, an auto body mechanic discovered the car had a gas leak that could have caught on fire or exploded at any moment.

Could a spirit possibly have influenced the person to give my friend the concert tickets knowing that he would get into a fender bender, which would lead to the discovery of the gas leak? I've seen too many coincidences that had significant results like this to not believe that this is how spirits work.

In a final example, I was once working on an important article and got stuck on which direction to take it. One night, while out with friends, a friend suggested I read the book *The Razor's Edge*. He thought it would help me. My friend was the messenger, but I didn't catch the message—or at least I didn't follow through with it. So when I didn't buy the book, my spirit guides used coincidence to emphasize the message. That same week, just three days after my friend suggested the book, my TiVo DVR "randomly" recorded *The Razor's Edge* movie. In case that wasn't clear, the doggone machine recorded the movie on its own. I watched the movie, and it turned out to be exactly what I needed to help me get past my writer's block.

This story is a great example of how our spirit guides don't just try once and give up. If we miss one opportunity to be guided, they continue trying until we get the message. But it sure helps if you stay aware of (1) your intuitive feelings, (2) the coincidences in your life, (3) the messages brought to you by messengers, and (4) the events that are attempting to lead you in new directions. If you do, you'll be helping your spirit guides to guide you, and you'll be a whole lot better off for it.

—◦◦◦—

What's an ascended master?

An ascended master is a spiritually advanced being who has completed the process of ascension and is filled with such wisdom and awareness that they no longer need to incarnate. As a result of their spiritual enlightenment, they now place themselves in the service of spirits who are having human experiences.

Some people refer to ascended masters as elders. I had an experience that allowed me to experience firsthand what it is like to be in an elder's presence. It was during one of my life-between-lives regressions where I was regressed into the spirit world while between lives. At first, I was regressed into a past life, but when I died in that past life, the regressionist guided me beyond that lifetime as I returned to the afterlife. Once on the other side, I experienced the life review process following that most recent lifetime.

This experience was absolutely breathtaking. First of all, I was in the spirit world, which is everything near-death experiencers say it is. I felt immense love, warmth, safety, and peace like I have never experienced in my lifetime. I had no desire to return my consciousness back to my prior life's body. That would have been like coming inside to a warm house filled with friends during a bitter-cold winter storm and then choosing to go back into the blizzard. So there I was, tranquilly absorbing this spirit-world scene when, suddenly, sitting before me was a group of seven advanced beings who emanated love and wisdom beyond measure and who promised to answer all my worldly questions. I was told (telepathically) that they were the Council of Elders.

So these seven beings of light, who were high-level spiritual masters (ascended masters), sat around an oval table with me. Although they were only masses of light in appearance, I still had a slight knowing of their personalities, their bodylike movements, and the most overwhelming sense that they loved me deeply. Their love was so intense that I burst into tears the moment I first felt it during the regression. Once in front of the Council of Elders, I immediately felt that they did not judge me for the errors of my past life. In fact, I felt their parentlike compassion for me because I was harshly judging myself.

While in their presence, I underwent my life review, experiencing my previous life all over again, but with crystal clarity of the triumphs and failures I had made during that lifetime. I learned lessons that have still not escaped me many years later, and I will never forget meeting these seven ascended masters.

So there are many different ascended masters of various descriptions or names. My experience with the elders is just one of many possibilities.

If you ever want to have an experience with ascended masters, channelers (as opposed to psychics or mediums) are the people who can communicate with them. A reading with a channeler, or a channeling demonstration in front of an audience, is not typically an evidence-based experience like with mediums, but it's a whole new level of experience that I highly recommend.

—⟡—

What do we look like in the spirit world?

We can choose to look like whatever we want as spirits. However, when spirits show themselves to a medium who is giving a reading to their loved ones, most people in spirit will show themselves in a way that their family will best identify them. This is also true if a loved one in spirit visits you in a dream.

What we need to remember, though, is that our loved ones are more likely to show themselves in a reading or dream as healthy as opposed to sick or injured. Who wants to be remembered as sick or injured, right? Therefore, even if they died appearing old and ailing, they are unlikely to visit you in a dream looking that way. If necessary, for the purposes of being identified, they might show a medium that they looked old and ailing when they died, but they will often let the medium know that they are not this way any longer. For their sake and yours, they want everyone to know that they are healthy and vibrant in their spiritual bodies.

As I've mentioned elsewhere, the truth is that people in spirit don't need to look like anyone since our true nature in spirit is energy and light. Many people who have had near-death experiences have said that they saw people in spirit as beings of light. Interestingly, even if you died and met a friend in spirit who you only saw as a being of light, you would still be able to identify her as your friend. And if you or she preferred, she could also show herself to you as she appeared in her human body.

It's helpful to keep in mind that we, as souls (rather than spirits), have each lived hundreds or thousands of lives. So we can choose the appearance of any one of those human bodies we've inhabited. That's pretty cool when you think about it.

At the same time, since we can be, do, and have anything we desire while in the spirit world, we could also choose to appear in any way we desire. Not that we would fool anyone with an alternate appearance since our identity would easily be recognized from our energy and light signature alone, but it gives us unlimited options on what we can look like, at least.

—m—

What age are we in the spirit world?

The truth is that there is no age in the afterlife. Our "souls" are eternal beings. With that understanding, though, the "spirit" of a person will often tell a medium during a reading that they imagine themselves at an age when they felt the most vitality and joy during their human life, which typically is anywhere from 20 to 40 years old.

After the initial reintegration back into the afterlife, however, age is entirely insignificant. Since there is no time or distance in the after-life, we don't have an age. We, as souls, are eternal beings that never get older and never die. Age and death are merely physical concepts that souls only experience while having a physical life. In fact, it's one of the reasons having a human life is so intriguing to spirits—mortal-ity changes everything.

—m—

Are children who died still children in the spirit world?

If you understood my answers to the last two questions, then it's probably obvious to you now that the answer is both yes and no. Yes, the spirit of the child will always relate to its human life as a child. So it will always identify itself as the child it was when it shows itself to a medium during a reading or in a dream visitation. Having never grown older than a child, there will always be that child within it.

Being a child is the essence of that spirit's human experience, so it remains as such for all eternity.

At the same time, the answer is also no. Once the child is in the spirit world again, it has the maturity of a soul as that is what we all are. Therefore, the spirit who was a child during its last physical life remembers its true nature as the ageless, timeless spiritual being that it is, yet without ever losing the experience and memories of its human lifetime as a child.

—⁂—

Will I retain my personality in the spirit world?

Interestingly enough, while there are many characteristics of our personality that are solely associated with our physical bodies and human egos, there are just as many that carry over from one lifetime to another and into the spirit world. You might call this our soul's signature personality. This is why we can have a past-life regression and still recognize our sibling, parent, or friend from our current life, even though they play a different role and might be the opposite sex in that past life.

When I've been regressed to past lives, I knew that my sister in one life was my wife in my current life. It was evident as a knowing, but it was also evident by looking at her eyes. Apparently, the eyes really are a window to the soul. And there are other signature characteristics as well.

Children have been known to have past-life memories and say things like "Mommy, Grandma isn't your mommy. She's my mommy and your sister." It's not that these kids are confused. They are just recalling the relationships from their previous lifetime. Since they have not been away from the spirit world for long, some children retain these memories in their early years of life. Eventually, though, these memories dissipate and are forgotten, but the point is that these children recognized these people from one life to another.

Because there are aspects of our personality and identity that are soul-based, there is never an issue of not recognizing a loved one even when they are in a new body in a past or future life. This is probably why we often meet someone for the first time and feel like we've known them forever. It's likely that we shared a past life together, or we know them from the spirit world.

None of what I just explained, however, changes the fact that a loved one's personality from this lifetime always stays intact as part of that person's soul. In other words, the life we are each living now, including our personalities and every memory we'll ever have, becomes part of our soul's makeup.

So when our loved ones in the spirit world show themselves to a medium during a reading or show themselves to us in a dream or vision, they are exactly as we remembered them—personality, appearance, and all. We just need to keep in mind that they will likely show themselves in a healthy state, even though they were ill or injured the last time we saw them.

—\~\~—

What does it feel like to be a spiritual being?

People in spirit who have communicated through mediums, people who have had near-death experiences, and even people who have experienced the spirit world during a life-between-lives regression all agree that there are no human words to fully describe what it's like to be in spirit form or be in the spirit world. All the same, this is what we know.

One of the first things people notice is how incredibly liberating it feels to be outside of the physical body. If you remember, as a child, being trapped inside a heavy Halloween costume and mask for a day, you get the gist of what it feels like for a spirit to be in a physical body, although that image doesn't nearly do it justice. One of the challenges to our spirit when choosing a physical life is knowing that it will be confined within a body. So it feels fantastic when it is free again.

Next, the feeling of weightlessness is frequently mentioned as one of the first things we notice and enjoy. The ability to float around unencumbered, controlling where we want to go with our mind, is apparently extraordinary.

We are light. There are no limits. Simply think of your grandmother in spirit, and you're with her. Think of your husband on earth, and you're with him. Think of a Hawaiian beach, and you're sitting on it. Think of the planet Mars, and you're exploring it. We have no limits as spiritual beings. We can float around like a helium balloon in the clouds or a hawk over the Grand Canyon. The experience of existing as a being of light is like no other.

Then there is the sense of peacefulness. We have no worries, no stress, and no fears as spiritual beings. The sense of inner peace is awesome. We are no longer a slave to our regrets of the past or our fears about the future. Present-moment awareness is built into the spiritual experience. All that exists is now, and everything in the now is perfect.

Since we are beings of light, the bright light of the Universe moves through us, oozing through our aura like the sun's rays filtering through the atmosphere on a clear day. We feel this light's love for us. We feel more deeply connected to it, and to one another, than is even possible as human beings. We feel completely protected by the light.

Because we feel loved, safe, and connected, and we are living so peacefully in the present moment of the afterlife, we feel nothing but joy. In fact, we are drunk with joy. And this happiness encompasses all that we do. It drives our decisions. It affects our relationships. It encourages playfulness.

This is not to say that spiritual life is a constant vacation. We work. We learn. We grow. And we deal with the errors of our most recent life. But we do this in a loving, joyful, safe, and peaceful environment. Being light is our true nature. So while words cannot nearly describe it with any real accuracy, this is what it feels like to be in spirit.

—∿—

How do spiritual beings communicate with other spiritual beings?

This is just another one of the bonuses of spiritual life. We communicate through our thoughts. There is no need for talking. There is no miscommunication, no misinterpretation of our words, and no misunderstandings. Communication is pure. And since other people in spirit can read our thoughts, there is only honesty, truth, and authenticity. People in spirit cannot tell a lie.

Being that there is no distance in the spirit world, two spirits can communicate regardless of what they are doing or where they are. I could be overlooking a waterfall in Venezuela and you could be watching polar bears in Greenland, yet we could have a conversation at the same moment. Of course, this is where it gets rather complicated from a technical standpoint because spirits can be in more than one place at a time. Therefore, you and I (as spirits) could have a conversation together while peering at the Eiffel Tower, and at the same time, I could be in Venezuela by the waterfall and you could be in Greenland with the polar bears.

When we die here in this lifetime and return home to the spirit world for our homecoming celebration, we might still imagine ourselves with a physical body and think we are talking with our mouths. But at some moment during the party, we're likely to notice that our loved ones already know what we're going to say before we say it. At this point, we'll probably smile and say, "Oh, I get it. You can read my mind. I was wondering why I knew what you were saying and your mouth wasn't moving." This is when we'll stop talking with our mouths because it is much easier and faster to just converse with our thoughts.

—⚍—

What if a spirit at a lower level wants to communicate with a spirit at a higher level?

Because we, as spiritual beings, vibrate at different frequencies, it is generally believed that we congregate with other spiritual beings of the same frequency (like attracts like), which translates into different levels of the spirit world.

In light of this, it's said that spirits can visit levels lower than their level (lower vibrations), but not visit higher levels (higher vibrations).

But that's not to say that we can't communicate with spirits of a higher level.

All we need to do is call upon another person in spirit who is of a higher level, and they will come to us, just as we will go to spirits who are at levels lower than our own. So communication is never an issue. Just think of the person in spirit with whom you wish to connect, and they'll instantly be aware of your call to them.

The only difference the levels make is that we must wait until we have increased our spiritual awareness and wisdom, and therefore our vibrational frequency, before we can travel to higher levels on our own. This is just one of the many motivations for ongoing spiritual growth in the spirit world. But communication between levels is never really an issue.

There is really no hierarchy or social structure that makes one soul better than another soul just because she is of a higher vibrational level. It's more about resonance, not class or limitation. No soul is being restrained from entering a level by any outside force. A lower-frequency soul simply won't have an attraction to the higher-frequency level because it won't resonate with him. So I wouldn't get too caught up or confused by the idea of levels in the spirit world because they don't mean what we humans would normally think levels mean.

—⁓—

Do people in spirit attend their own funerals?

Yes, people in spirit attend their own funerals, but probably not for the reasons that most people would assume. Spirits are primarily interested in helping their loved ones who are grieving. They want to ease their loved ones' feelings of loss and heartache. And they want to make their presence felt, if possible, so the bereaved know they are still around them.

People in spirit are not interested in who does and does not show up at their funeral. They are not concerned about their popularity. But they do like their life to be remembered and honored. And they appreciate knowing that people loved them (and still love them). Every life is significant and purposeful, and it helps those in spirit to witness this memorial "celebration of their life" as opposed to the mourning of their death.

People in spirit also attend their own funerals (and memorial services) because they feel the love that those in attendance radiate for them. Since the most important quality of life is love, it increases a spirit's vibration to feel the love being expressed at such services, which helps them with their own spiritual evolvement.

We all love to be loved, and funeral services are the perfect venue to express your love for your recently deceased loved one before settling back into the distractions of your day-to-day life. Always know that your deceased loved ones are present with you at their funeral, just as they are present with you whenever you think of them. So sharing happy memories of them with others at any time is a wonderful way to honor their life.

—⚹—

Does my loved one in spirit see everything I do, even in the shower and bedroom?

My wife, Melissa, asked me this question early in my investigation into the afterlife. I laughed when she first told me she was concerned that deceased loved ones could see her in the shower. Then I got to thinking about it and became somewhat disturbed by the idea myself.

The answer is yes; our loved ones can see everything we do, even in the bathroom and bedroom. But they have no interests of a physical nature now that they are in spirit, and they are fully respectful of our privacy. Keep in mind that people in spirit have about as much interest in watching you run around naked as you do watching your cat or dog run around naked—in other words, none. They no longer have any attachment to the flesh.

105

I'm sure that some people are concerned that their deceased husband or wife might see them in the bedroom with their new lover. And it's fully understandable why that would be an unsettling situation. What you want to keep in mind is that people in spirit have no desire to watch us do the hokeypokey. They are going to know you have a lover as there is no avoiding that, but they aren't going to be watching you with high-powered binoculars. In fact, they aren't going to watch you, period.

While on this subject, I should point out that people on the other side always want their spouses to move on and find love again. They are not going to feel jealous. Jealousy doesn't exist in spirit; that's a human condition. They want you to love and be loved during your life here. So as long as that's the kind of relationship you have with someone, your deceased spouse or lover is going to be happy that you have someone to express your love with physically as well as emotionally.

—���—

How can I assure my privacy from loved ones in spirit?

If it will make you feel any better, people in spirit abide by our requests. So tell your deceased loved ones in spirit that you don't want them seeing you in awkward ways. Be as specific as you wish. You can specify to them where they are not invited. But don't give these instructions to your *spirit guides* just in case you slip in the shower and need some help. There's nothing handier than a competent spirit guide creating coincidences and miracles for your rescue. So give spirit guides full reign while giving loved ones in spirit their boundaries.

—���—

Is there anything I can do to help my loved one in spirit?

You can honor your loved ones by keeping their memories alive. For example, keep their photos around the house. If you don't currently have any framed, pick out one or two good ones, and get them framed for your wall or mantle. It's nice for you and them to keep them a part of your life in this way.

As mentioned earlier in this book, talk with your loved ones in spirit whenever you think of them. In many cases, the thought of them will likely pop into your mind if they've dropped by to see you. So if you find yourself suddenly thinking about your deceased spouse, parent, grandparent, sibling, child, or friend for no apparent reason, it's probably because they've shown up. Acknowledge them whenever you think this is the case. Tell them what's happening in your life and in your other family members' lives, and talk to them just like they had dropped in on you for a visit when they were physically alive because they are still spiritually alive. You might even ask them if they have any messages for you and then just be aware of what thoughts randomly pop into your head.

Although it might be difficult for you, your loved ones are not going to mind if you discard or give away some of their belongings that are only taking up space in your home or life. In the same way, people in spirit are happy to see you redecorate their bedroom or office. Perhaps you could turn it into something that will benefit you, like a library, sewing room, TV room, or billiards room. They will be thrilled that you transformed the room into something that brings you joy. Our loved ones in spirit live in the present moment, so they certainly don't want us to live in the past. Keeping their bedroom, office, or workshop exactly as it was when they left it—like some kind of museum or shrine—is not anything they desire.

It's also healthy for you to talk to your deceased loved ones about any issues between the two of you, even though you can't likely see or hear them. I mentioned earlier in this book that our deceased loved ones are in the room when we talk to them, so just go ahead and talk right out loud to them. Tell them what they did and how that made you feel, and express any anger, resentment, or other emotions you might be feeling toward them.

Your loved ones in spirit are going to fully understand what you're saying since they were able to know firsthand how they hurt you when they experienced their life review. So it's good therapy for you and them to discuss these issues privately when you're ready to do so. I wish more people realized that their opportunity to work things out with people doesn't end with someone's passing.

This is a useful exercise because our loved ones in spirit seek our forgiveness. Once they arrived in the afterlife and had their life review, they saw everything about their life from an entirely new perspective. They saw the errors of their ways, so they know where they fell short or even failed. At the same time, they understand why you might have fallen short or even failed in reference to your relationship with them too, and therefore, they forgive you for anything you might have done or failed to do. This is why having a conversation with them can be helpful to both of you, even though it will likely seem like a one-way conversation.

—◊—

Do prayers have any positive effect for our loved ones in spirit?

There is a great deal of evidence to suggest that prayers (intentions) actually permeate Universal Energy and have a real effect. So when we pray for a loved one who has passed, our prayers are heard and fulfilled. A simple prayer for their safe and peaceful entry back into the spirit world can actually raise our deceased loved one's energy for that purpose. While it is also true that people will cross over to the other side safely and peacefully without anyone's prayers, especially considering that many dying people don't have anyone to pray for them, our prayers are always welcomed and appreciated by our loved ones. It's like adding a little fuel to their tank.

PART FIVE

—∽—

QUESTIONS ABOUT THE WANTS AND NEEDS OF SPIRITS

How long does my loved one in spirit want me to grieve?

Your loved one in spirit doesn't want you to grieve at all, if it could be avoided. They want you to be at peace and live the rest of your life as joyfully as possible. But since grief is a natural process that is necessary in order to come to terms (reach acceptance) with the fact that our loved ones have passed, your loved one wants you to grieve for however long is necessary for you. That might be a month, or that might be five years. While it pains them to see you suffering due to their loss any longer than necessary, they understand that we all must endure the bereavement process when someone passes. But they hope we will heal and move on to live our lives fully the moment we feel ready.

What's important to understand is that your grief does not honor your deceased loved one. Said another way, they do not gain or benefit in any way by your mourning, and they are not flattered by it. So do not prolong your suffering simply because you think your loved one in spirit prefers it. They already know that you love and miss them. They don't need you to prolong your sorrow, heartache, and misery in order to prove it.

—⟋⟍—

How does my spouse in spirit feel about me getting remarried?

One of the most common messages from people in spirit to their surviving spouses through mediums is that they want them to find love again and remarry. I have witnessed this in hundreds of readings during medium demonstrations where mediums give readings while onstage to people in the audience. I have never heard the opposite message. They always encourage their spouses to get married again.

Even if your deceased loved one was a jealous human being when alive, this changes once they are back in the spirit world. People are able to see the bigger picture in the afterlife. They realize that there is nothing more important than love. And they want their spouses to know love as fully as possible during this short journey on the earth plane.

Jealousy is a trait of the human ego, not spirit. It feeds off imaginary thoughts of separation, competition, and fear. Therefore, jealousy cannot and does not exist in the afterlife because there is no separation, competition, or fear in the light. There is only love, which is what our loved ones in spirit want for us.

What we mistakenly believe here as human beings is that love is in limited supply. So we often think that if someone loves us, then there is no room for them to love another, or if they do love another, then they must somehow love us less because people only have so much love to give. This, of course, is an erroneous illusion.

People in spirit realize that love is unlimited. They know that their spouse on earth is not going to love them any less by falling in love with another person. They feel no threat in this regard. And since they love their surviving spouse unconditionally, they only want to see them happy. So they are always pleased to learn that there is someone new in their spouse's life who makes that person feel loved again to the point of wanting to marry them.

—⁓—

How does my child in spirit feel about me having another child?

Just as I mentioned with spouses in spirit, children in spirit know that your loving another child will not diminish your love for them. Therefore, your child in spirit would be pleased to see you have another child. They want to see you giving love and being loved because love is what is important. People in spirit, regardless of what age they died, always want their loved ones here on the physical plane to be happy and loving as much as possible.

Keep in mind that our souls have no age. We have likely lived thousands of human lives. Therefore, even when we die on the physical plane as children, we return to the spirit world as mature souls of great wisdom. With this wisdom, our souls recognize that our parents on earth will always love us regardless of how many more children they choose to have.

Children who have died and then come through in readings of spirit communication always express pleasure that their parents are having another child. Don't forget that your deceased child likely met your new child before you did—since they met in the spirit world prior to your new child's birth—even in cases where your new child is adopted.

Of course, the bigger picture is that you all met before any of you were born. In most cases, you planned that the first child was going to return to the spirit world early and the second child was going to show up later—if you choose to allow it.

—⁓—

Does my loved one in spirit want me to solve his/her crime? Does my loved one in spirit want justice?

People in spirit have no use for justice except when it will help their surviving loved ones feel better. So no, they do not seek justice, and they do not care if their crime is solved unless it will somehow benefit the people they love on the earth plane. Let me illustrate how this might happen.

For example, if a mother is suffering because she thinks her daughter died by suicide (which is considered a sin in this mother's religion), yet the daughter was actually murdered, then the spirit of the daughter has a reason to want her crime solved—she wants her mother to know that she didn't take her own life.

As a second example, if a man went missing because he was robbed and left for dead while taking a walk after an argument with his spouse (and his body was never found), he might want his crime solved so that his wife knows that he didn't run out on her or that he didn't take his own life because of the argument.

From a spirit-world perspective, the only purpose in having crimes solved is to reduce the suffering of those still living. Otherwise, the truth of every crime will eventually be known since we'll all find out what really happened once we die and return to the here-after. And since there is no concept of time in the afterlife, people in spirit don't feel like they have to wait long for their loved ones to learn the truth about their crimes, so there is no rush for the truth to be known. Most spirits say it's like a blink of an eye before all their loved ones are with them again on the other side.

Many times, a crime is left unsolved because it serves the best inter-est of the people living. What I mean by this is that it fulfills those people's pre-birth plans to have this experience. Why? Because not knowing if your son took his own life or was murdered, for example, is a very challenging human experience.

Each possibility holds different meaning to the surviving loved ones, so they don't know what to think or how to deal with it when the mystery is left unsolved. Yet this alone is an experience that a soul might choose to know, so the mystery might go unsolved forever, or the mystery might eventually be solved—depending upon the soul's desires.

—⁂—

Does my loved one in spirit seek vengeance?

Vengeance is a human concept that does not exist in the afterlife. It's of a lower energy, much like jealousy, hatred, and fear. Such negative thoughts are impossible for spirits living in the light of the Universe. Thus, no person in spirit would ever desire it.

People in spirit know only love. As a result, they actually believe in the idea of turning the other cheek. They know that two wrongs do not make a right, and therefore, two acts of hatred can never make an act of love. So vengeance is something they never desire. Instead, they prefer forgiveness—you forgiving any person who might have been responsible for that person's death or for harming them during their human life. It's not an easy task for many people, but that's what spiritual growth is all about.

Forgiveness is actually less about letting the other person off the hook than it is relieving yourself of suffering. When you carry the weight of blaming someone with contempt, it is actually your burden to carry. But when you release them of that blame and contempt, you release yourself of holding that negative energy inside you, which raises your overall vibration of love.

—⁂—

Would my loved one in spirit like me to create a foundation in his/her name?

People in spirit are pleased to be remembered. Even in the afterlife, people like knowing that those they left behind still love and remember them. So in this way, it is a loving gesture to create a foundation in your deceased loved one's name. If it is also helping people (or some positive cause) in some way, as most foundations do, that's an added bonus.

At the same time, no spirit specifically wishes that someone would create a foundation in their name. Only do it if it is something that you feel called to do. The last thing a person in spirit wants is for their loved one on the earth plane to feel burdened by an obligation to do something in their name. Creating a foundation requires a lot of time and effort, so you should only do it if it makes *you* feel good—for instance, if it gives you a sense of purpose. There are plenty of other nice gestures you can make in their memory that require much less effort.

On the other hand, creating a foundation in your deceased loved one's name can be a wonderful exercise to heal your grief. For many, creating a foundation of this sort can turn a loss into something positive, such as a foundation that helps people or a cause. This can help to give that person's passing a sense of meaning—"At least his death led to saving lives," or "Her passing was the catalyst for supporting children with a talent in music." And if this helps you to move forward after loss, it serves both you and others, plus your loved one in spirit is happy that you're happy.

—⟡—

My loved one and I never discussed it. Did I make the right choice to cremate (or not cremate)? How do I know if my loved one in spirit wants me to keep his/her ashes or spread them somewhere?

Once people leave their bodies and return home to the spirit world, they have no attachment to their bodies. Whether you bury their body or cremate it is of no significance. They also have no attachment to whether you bury their cremated ashes in a gravesite, scatter them at some memorable location, or keep them in an urn on your mantle. And they don't mind if you separate their ashes and give them to several different people.

What's important to your loved one in spirit is that you do what gives you the most peace and comfort. If cremation is less expensive and, therefore, creates less of a financial burden on you, your loved one will be happy with that choice. If you personally prefer a casket and gravesite because it gives you a location to visit and remember them, then that too is a wonderful choice. If, however, you feel more comforted to know that your loved one's ashes are in the house with you, then once again, your loved one in spirit will be happy with that idea too.

There is no right or wrong from the perspective of the person in spirit when it comes to burial choices. And since there is no religion in the afterlife, even those spirits who were strict followers of a particular religion (here on the physical plane) no longer concern themselves with the rituals of their earthly religion. They still honor *your* religious choices because that is what gives you peace of mind. But the one true faith in spirit is simply love.

—⚒—

Is my loved one in spirit satisfied with his/her gravestone (headstone)?

I assume that, by now, you're beginning to get the idea that your loved one in spirit only wants what is best for you. Once a person has passed and gone to the afterlife, they have no personal feelings around the size of their gravestone, the type of stone, the shape of the stone, or the words written on the stone. Whatever choice you make regarding the headstone is perfect in their mind.

Just as I wrote about the choice to bury or cremate, your loved one in spirit only wants what is best for you. They do not want you to spend more than you can afford as that would be an unnecessary burden. The only thing that is important is the gesture of remembrance and love. Therefore, you simply cannot go wrong in this regard.

When my father passed in 1997, my mother, sister, and I did not have the financial means to purchase a headstone for my father's cemetery plot. Five years later, I had the means and desire, so I finally bought his headstone. Through medium readings, my father expressed his appreciation for the stone and his appreciation that we waited until the time was right for us—financially—to purchase it. Because of my investigations into the afterlife, I knew that my father didn't care about it either way. But I knew it was important to my mother that my father has a headstone. And since it was important to my mom, it was important to my dad, especially since my mother likes to visit the gravesite, put flowers on it, and so forth.

I don't want to miscommunicate the important message here, so let me clarify. Our deceased loved ones want to be remembered. Of course, it is their spirit who wants to be remembered, not their soul. Their soul is detached, but their spirit is still that personality we remember, only much more enlightened.

This means that they care to be remembered and to have their life celebrated. But having a few photographs around the house or wearing the necklace he gave you or wearing your father's watch is sufficient. They certainly love the meaning behind a gravestone and will cherish the words you have engraved on it (if you do that). But it's your memory of them that matters, not the stone. The headstone is just a stone located in a field (cemetery) that probably meant nothing to them when physically alive. So burial rituals and markers honor the memory of our passed loved ones, but only if it is something that works in your favor as well.

—◊—

How often does my loved one in spirit want me to visit his/her gravesite?

Our loved ones in spirit like to be remembered, but they have no specific desires around how we remember them. So it doesn't matter to them if you visit their gravesite or not. They want you to remember them in the manner that works best for you.

Consequently, if you live in California but your father is buried in Massachusetts, your father has no interest in you flying to New England once a year just to visit his gravesite unless that is a ritual that you enjoy and can afford (both in time and travel costs). If it's something that you like to do, it's a nice ceremony in his memory. And if it gets you back East to see family members and friends, it serves that purpose as well. But your father doesn't mind if you go there or not provided you take time out to think of him in some way. If you simply take the time to visit your favorite place in nature that is local to your home and think about him, that alone is enough.

A common misconception is that our deceased loved ones are hanging out at the cemetery by their gravesite. It's simply not true. As I've written elsewhere in this book, the spirit world is a dimension that exists all around us, and spirits can be in multiple places at one time. So they will always be present with you when you visit their gravesite, but you do not need to go there in order to talk with them. If you're not there, they're not there either.

I've always been amused by mediums who claim to see spirits at cemeteries. You often witness these claims during Halloween specials on television. In my opinion, it's a misleading fallacy to spread. Can you imagine this idea that our loved ones in spirit are somehow tethered to their gravesites to spend eternity at the cemetery? That would be horrible. And of course, it's not true. Cemeteries are where the bodies of dead people are buried, but their spirit (consciousness) is in the spiritual dimension, where they are free to go anywhere they please.

—ɷ—

Is it okay to split my loved one's ashes so that other family members can spread them somewhere?

Yes, as mentioned earlier, your loved one has no attachment to her body, so the ashes are merely a symbol of her memory. If you want to split up her ashes so that several people can remember her in this way, your loved one will feel honored and loved by the gesture. You are not affecting their spirit or soul by separating the ashes. The spirit has absolutely no connection to those ashes other than what they mean symbolically to the surviving loved ones.

—⁄∿⁄—

Does my loved one in spirit want a funeral (memorial service)?

Our loved ones in spirit are happy that we want to celebrate their lives and have a ceremony in their memory. Such services are meaningful to them. Funerals and memorial services are traditional ceremonies that are set up to do this, so they are a perfect ritual for this purpose.

Funerals and memorials are also designed to help us—the surviving loved ones—say goodbye. Directors of funeral parlors or religious leaders traditionally organize them. These helpful services take the pressure off us to organize such a gathering when we are already overwhelmed by grief. But they are not the only option.

As I've written in other answers within this section, our deceased loved ones only want what is best for us. If we can't afford a traditional funeral service, which can be quite costly, our loved ones don't want us to get into debt in order to have it. Any ceremony—be it at your home, by the ocean, or on a mountain—is appropriate. Design it to be meaningful and beautiful, but it doesn't have to be costly or complicated. What is important is the sentiment behind it.

The eulogy, remembrances, and prayers are what fill our loved ones in spirit with our love. The flowers, funeral processions, caskets, and cemetery plots can be nice, but these are matters of the physical world. A simple cookout or outing by the lake where people get to share memories of the deceased is quite sufficient. I once attended a memorial service at an art studio where the deceased's artwork was displayed. It was beautiful. And anyone who had memories to share about the man in spirit told their stories. It was both meaningful and personal.

—◊◊—

Does my loved one in spirit forgive me?

When a person dies and returns home to the hereafter, they see the bigger picture of human interaction. They recognize *why* you said and did certain things, not just *what* you said or did. Because of this enhanced perspective and their freedom from the physical ways of being (which include the ego), they always find it in their heart to forgive. Forgiveness is an act of love, and our loved ones in spirit always act out of love.

In most cases, our emotional reactions are motivated by past experiences with other people. If a woman suddenly gets angry with her husband for forgetting her birthday, for example, her anger might stem from memories of her parents forgetting to pick her up after school when she was seven years old. There she sat waiting for hours, scared and alone, possibly interpreting the mishap as her parents not loving her. And if this sort of experience happened multiple times during her childhood, it could certainly affect her relationships later in life.

Thirty years later, when her spouse forgets her birthday for the third time, she overreacts in such a way that possibly leads to a divorce. Subconsciously, the husband's forgetfulness leads her to believe he doesn't love her. And in an effort to shield herself from the pain she recalls from her childhood, she divorces him in avoidance of her heart being broken.

When the ex-husband passes and is now in spirit, he now sees with clarity why his former wife responded the way she did to his forgetfulness. He not only understands, but he also has deep compassion for her. As a result, he forgives her wholeheartedly.

I have witnessed a lot of people's readings with mediums, many at public events known as medium demonstrations. Many people ask the medium if their deceased loved one forgives them, and not once have I ever witnessed a person in spirit not forgiving the person getting the reading.

As I wrote earlier in this book, forgiveness is less about letting the other person off the hook than it is relieving oneself of suffering. When you carry the weight of blaming someone with contempt, it is actually your burden to carry. But when you release them of that blame and contempt, you release yourself of holding that negative energy inside you, which raises your overall vibration of love.

Our loved ones in spirit know this better than we can. And because they are beings of light and love, they are not equipped to hold the lower energies of anger, blame, and contempt. They forgive us because it is not in their nature to not forgive.

They also forgive us because of what I'll call our human ignorance—we don't know what we don't know. To them, we are like children with so much more to learn. This is not our fault; it's the nature of our species. Just as we forgive children for their words or actions because they don't know any better, spirits forgive us for the same reason. We make choices and have reactions because we are humans. It's simply part of the human experience.

—⚬—

Does my loved one in spirit want me to forgive him/her?

Yes, people in spirit appreciate our forgiveness. They don't want anything they did or said to stand in the way of our love for them. Now that they are in spirit, they have a spiritual-realm perspective regarding their human choices and actions. They see everything with greater clarity.

Once they arrived in the afterlife and had their life review, they were able to feel how you felt when they spoke or acted in ways that hurt you mentally, physically, or emotionally. They saw the errors of their ways, so they know where they fell short or even failed. At the same time, they understand why you might have fallen short or failed in reference to your relationship with them too, and therefore, they forgive you for anything you might have done or failed to do.

As mentioned elsewhere in this book, they also want you to forgive them for your sake. When you stop holding on to your negative feelings toward them, you relieve yourself of holding those lower energies inside you. So your forgiveness toward others actually brings you inner peace. Holding grudges actually does more harm to you than to those whom you direct that anger toward. Thus, your loved ones in spirit seek your forgiveness for your sake as well as their own.

—ɷ—

We argued shortly before her death; is she still angry with me?

If you've read the last few answers in this book, you've learned that spirits view us much like we view children. In this way, just as you would forgive your child for saying something out of anger toward you (because they're simply acting from emotion), our loved ones in spirit instantly let go of any negative words we said to them prior to their passing. They recognize that we are emotional beings and that we often say things we don't mean.

Those in spirit can feel our love for them. They can read our thoughts. They can connect with us in ways that they never could as humans. So they already know how you feel about them. And they don't want you to suffer over concerns about silly words that you said in anger. I recommend that you just let it go and forgive yourself for what was said in the past.

Likewise, you should not ruminate about anything your loved said before their passing. It's human to argue. The only reason it bothers you so much now is because they passed before you had the opportunity to make amends. But if you've gotten this far in this book, you now realize that your loved one is not holding any grudges toward you in the spirit world.

Plus you know they understand exactly how you feel. And if you're not 100 percent sure, talk to them out loud, and tell them how you feel. Do it right now, if you want. Let them know how their words made you feel. Get whatever you need to say off your chest. And then let it go—release that from your aura. Even better, if you can find it in your heart, forgive first and then forget.

PART SIX

—⚉—

QUESTIONS ABOUT SPIRIT COMMUNICATION

Can my loved one in spirit hear me when I talk or pray to him/her?

Our loved ones in spirit always hear us when we talk or pray to them. They express this through mediums all the time. All we need to do is think of them, and they are instantly aware of our thoughts. This includes talking out loud to them.

But our loved ones in spirit are also aware of when we write a letter or email to them, even if we have no place to send it. They know when we're talking about them with someone else. They know when we draw a picture for them or make a birthday card for them or sing a song for them. And they know when we're simply looking at a picture of them and thinking about past memories with them.

—⚮—

Why can't I see or hear my loved one in spirit?

People living on the spiritual plane vibrate at a much higher frequency than we do. Being on the physical plane, we vibrate at a lower, denser frequency, which results in our inability to see or hear spirits (until we learn how to access and develop our psychic and mediumistic abilities).

It's a common teaching that in order to communicate with spirits, we must raise our vibration (usually through meditation), and spirits must lower their vibration in order to create a link or connection where we are able to hear, see, or feel them. This is why people who follow a daily meditation practice often realize at some point that they are more intuitive and begin to either hear, feel, or see spirits (or all three). Meditation alone isn't always enough to develop one's abilities for this purpose, but it's a good start. Then one can take a class on psychic and mediumistic development in order to get to the next level.

Regardless of what some psychic mediums claim, no human being can see and hear spirits exactly the same way that we see and hear other human beings. It would be a very confusing world if we could. While I know that television shows and feature films often portray mediums talking to spirits as if the people in spirit were solid matter, in reality, mediums see spirits either in their mind's eye (they see pictures of them in fleeting thoughts) or as an apparition, which is less common. And even though the most experienced mediums will sometimes describe seeing spirits "as solid as you and I," they still recognize that the spirit is a spirit and not a human.

Most teachers of spirit communication will tell you that hearing spirits is easier than seeing them. In this case, what they are hearing is a faint and often distorted voice that many compare to listening to someone talking on a radio station with lots of static. However, most mediums are hearing these voices in their mind, which generally results in greater clarity, though some claim to actually hear spirits with their ears. For those who hear spirits in their mind, beginner mediums will typically hear their own voice saying the words of the spirit. Later, as one gets more advanced as a medium, they might begin to hear the tone and vernacular of the person in spirit (that is, the tone and vernacular they had as humans before they passed).

Seeing and hearing spirits is comparable to seeing and hearing people in your memories of them. Just as you can see your friend and hear what she said yesterday in your mind (your memory), this is how most spirit communication with mediums works. If you stop to remember, you can hear your friend's voice and what she said. You can hear her accent or vocal inflections. You can even see her walking, talking, and doing things. Well, this is similar to how most mediums communicate with people in spirit.

Finally, I should mention that many folks find it easier to "feel" their loved ones in spirit, meaning intuitively feeling their presence nearby. You've probably had this type of experience where you're in a room and, suddenly, you think of a loved one in spirit and get all tingly as if they're right there in the room with you. Sometimes you might even feel the hair on the back of your neck stand on end.

While you're not going to be able to prove your loved one's presence in the room, your energy body is picking up their vibe, which is sending a signal to your intuition. Even the skeptic in me can't deny when I feel this type of sensation at the same time that thoughts of my loved one fill my mind.

—◠◠◠—

Is there an appropriate time to communicate with loved ones in spirit?

You can communicate with your loved ones in spirit at any time. There is no inappropriate time to say hello or ask them for assistance, mostly because there is no concept of time in the spirit world. So whether you are talking out loud to them and trusting that they are in the room with you (because they are) or writing a letter to them and trusting that they are reading it as you write (because they are), your loved ones in spirit welcome you to do this at any hour, day or night.

—∽∿∾—

How often is it appropriate to talk to or call on my loved one in spirit?

My advice to you is to treat your loved ones in spirit the same way that you would treat your loved ones who are still alive. If your loved one died recently, it's expected that you'll feel the need to talk to them more often. But once the intensity of your grief has diminished, just communicate with them the same way you did when they were alive physically.

This is helpful for *you* too. You don't want to lean on their guidance or assistance for every little thing in your life. It's important that you learn to live your life without their constant help. Plus it isn't the job of your deceased loved ones to guide you in your day-to-day life. That is the job of your spirit guides. So if you want to tell your loved one in spirit about something wonderful that has occurred in your life, go right ahead. But refrain from asking them if you should turn right or left at every intersection in your life. If you feel the need for direction, make the request of your spirit guide (or guides) who have been guiding you since the day you were born. It's okay to ask your loved ones for help now and then. I certainly do. The point here is to remain balanced and not become dependent upon them.

Despite the idea of giving our loved ones in spirit some space from guiding our lives 24-7, I've heard hundreds of spirits convey through mediums that it's always appropriate to talk to them when you want to check in. If you want to tell them how much you miss them and love them, don't hold back—they love that. That's an important part of grieving, and who would ever get tired of being remembered, whether in physical or spiritual form?

—⟋⟍—

Is it wrong to ask my loved one in spirit to help me with little requests like finding my missing keys?

There is nothing wrong with asking for assistance from people in spirit, including requesting help to find your lost keys. But do keep in mind that most guidance is going to come from your spirit guides or Universal Intelligence, not your deceased loved ones.

The big-picture answer to this question is that you're only going to be guided to find your keys if and when you are meant to find them. If losing your keys is going to lead you in a direction you need to go in order to have an experience you're meant to have in life, then you won't find those keys no matter how much you ask for assistance—because the assistance you're getting from spirit is to not find them.

For example, losing your keys might make you late for a new job interview, which might then result in your not getting that job. If your spirit guides know that there is a better job coming in a few days or even weeks—one that is better for the growth of your soul—then losing your keys might be a result of spiritual guidance.

Losing your keys might also delay you enough so that you miss becoming involved in a car accident. Or it might delay you so that you cross paths with a very important person in your future. Or it might delay you enough to finally recognize that your stove is still on. Once you shut off the stove, you might then see your keys sitting on the counter.

So it's perfectly fine to ask your loved one in spirit for guidance. But if your request wasn't granted, just keep in mind that there might be a good reason for it. And don't forget that your spirit guides, who are helping you, are not always your loved ones in spirit, so it's good to send your everyday spirit guides gratitude too.

—⁂—

Can my loved ones in spirit visit me in my dreams?

You bet your loved ones can visit you in your dreams. This is called a dream visitation.

Thousands of people have experienced a dream visitation. In most cases, the dream is extremely vivid and feels like you are really in the presence of your loved one, which, of course, you are. And you often feel a heightened sense of emotion due to the reunion. While most dreams usually seem disjointed and filled with fantasy, dream visitations seem authentic, as if your spirit and your loved one's spirit have met in person.

It is easier for our loved ones to visit us in our dreams because our attention is withdrawn from our conscious, logical mind, and therefore, it's not available to be skeptical or scared. While sleeping, our minds are in the unconscious (subconscious) state, which is our connection to the spiritual realm. It is in this middle space between the physical realm and the spiritual realm that those in spirit can meet with us.

Those who have experienced a dream visitation say that they remember the details of the dream with great clarity many years later. They often remember the dream as if they had the dream the prior evening, even if the dream visitation was 20 years earlier. They also say that it was unlike most dreams that are symbolic or metaphorical; their dream visitation was straightforward and clear—their loved one in spirit wanted to comfort them.

The most common dream visitation scenario is that a loved one in spirit suddenly appears in a dream, and it's like the two of you are with one another again. Sometimes you'll be talking with your mouths, but sometimes you'll notice that you're communicating telepathically. Nonetheless, the conversation is usually brief and focused. Those in spirit generally want you to know that they still exist, that they are happy, healthy, and at peace, and that you don't need to worry about them. In some cases, you might be able to ask them a question and get an answer, but in most cases, they will leave after they have delivered what they want to say.

—⟋⟍—

Why did my loved one in spirit visit my sibling in a dream, but not me?

There's never any guarantee that your loved one in spirit will visit you in a dream, but you can certainly request it. Pray to your loved one, and ask if they could come to you while dreaming. If they know you're open to it and can handle it, it might happen.

Most people believe they would like to have a dream visitation, but you might not be as open to the experience as you think. For one, you must be open-minded enough in terms of skepticism to allow it. Skepticism can ward off such dreams simply because you don't believe it. Have you ever looked all over for your car keys or sunglasses only to realize that they were right in a spot you looked all along? Many people have had this experience, and it is because they didn't believe their keys or sunglasses were going to be in that spot, so they never even saw them. This is the power of skepticism.

Your loved ones in spirit know best if you might be scared by the experience of a dream visitation or confused by it. For example, if your religion has taught you that only demons visit people in their dreams, then your deceased loved one certainly isn't going to use this method to contact you. But if you are open-minded and wouldn't be scared by a visit from your loved one in your dreams, it is much more likely to occur. (By the way, in case you're wondering, I do not believe in demons as I've never seen any evidence that they exist.)

Your sibling might be more open to a dream visitation or might need it more. My guess is that it's not an easy task to show up in our dreams, so they are going to save it for those people who really need the experience. If your beliefs are such that you already know your loved one is okay, then it's not necessary that your loved one in spirit endure the extra effort to appear in your dream.

On the other hand, some people dream differently than others. For instance, I rarely ever remember my dreams. So it might be a big waste for one of my loved ones in spirit to visit me that way. Thus, who gets a dream visitation and who doesn't might depend on our dreaming habits. Some of us just might not dream appropriately for a dream visitation to be possible. If you're someone who never really sleeps very deeply, that might be an issue.

Finally, because the purpose of life is experience (as discussed in the "Big Picture" section at the beginning of this book), having a dream visitation might not be an experience your soul wants you to have. Every experience we have could lead us in a new direction. If your soul knows that you are more likely to stay on the path intended for your life by *not* having a dream visitation, then your soul won't allow it because it's in your best interest not to experience one. On the other hand, if having a dream visitation is an experience that will benefit your life's plan, then the possibility of having one is much greater.

In the end, I wouldn't take it personally that your loved one visited your sibling in her dream and not you. Look at the glass as half full, and be happy that your loved one showed up in anyone's dream. Now your family has had direct contact as evidence that your loved one happily exists in the afterlife. That's a wonderful gift regardless of who had the dream.

—⚹—

Should I get a reading with a psychic medium? How might a spirit communication reading benefit me?

If you are interested in reuniting with your loved one who has died, I highly recommend a reading of spirit communication with a psychic medium (often just called a medium). It can be one of the most en-lightening and rewarding experiences of your lifetime. Even for those of us who are open-minded but skeptical, a reading with a medium has the potential to provide strong evidence of life after death as well as evidence that your deceased loved one is not gone forever but rather fully alive in spirit.

For me, I initially sought out a medium in order to find out what happened to my father after he passed. I had many questions following his death, many of the same questions that I've answered in this book. So getting a reading with a medium started me on the path to obtaining these answers.

Naturally, I didn't get all my questions answered in my first reading or even my second or third. But the evidence I gained from my first reading was irrefutable. I knew that there was no way that this stranger (the medium) could know everything she was telling me without being in direct communication with my deceased father.

It turned out that my father's passing became a catalyst for my spiritual growth. His death led to my first reading with a medium, which led to my investigating the afterlife. Investigating the afterlife led to me having dozens of other enlightening experiences that taught me about life after death, including past-life regressions, life-between-lives regressions, spirit artistry sessions, meditation, and channeled readings as well as interviews with people who have had near-death experiences, deathbed visions, dream visitations, and past-life recall, to name just a few.

The first thing I learned from my investigation of the afterlife is that *we don't die*. As my investigations progressed, I discovered that *we are spiritual beings having a physical experience*. And still, later, I came to know that *we are all connected by the matrix that is the Universe*, including everyone of this world and everyone on the other side.

This all began because I had a reading with a psychic medium. So yes, I highly recommend the experience.

—∞—

What signals or communications might my loved one in spirit be trying to send me?

Most people in our society have never been to a psychic medium and probably never plan to visit one, so our loved ones in spirit need to let us know that they are still around us in other ways. It's important to those in spirit to help us with our grief as it pains them to see us suffer due to their loss. So they try to send us signals in our everyday experiences that will be comforting and reassuring that they're okay. These are called after-death communications (ADCs), a term coined by Bill and Judy Guggenheim, who wrote a groundbreaking book on this subject titled *Hello from Heaven*.

There are multiple signals or signs that spirits send to their loved ones here on the physical plane. I'll mention some of the most common ADCs.

Smelling a fragrance is a common after-death communication. If you've ever been in a room and the scent of your late father's cologne suddenly fills the room, it's probably an ADC if there's no logical reason for smelling it. Especially if you were just thinking about your father or talking about him when you smelled his cologne, this is his way of letting you know he's around.

The range of scents is unlimited. You might smell the scent of your deceased grandfather's pipe or the scent of banana bread, which might remind you of your late aunt. You might smell your mother's favorite flower, if she's in spirit, or the smell of tar if your departed brother worked for a company that paved driveways. The point of the scented ADC is that there is no logical way to account for the smell so that you know it's a signal from your deceased loved one that she is present.

Some people have actually seen visions of their loved one in spirit. The most common vision occurs when people wake up from sleep (or are falling off to sleep). This somber state of mind (like a deep meditation) is the best time for us to be able to see a spirit. In many of these cases, people see a vision of their loved ones at the end of their bed. But I've heard stories from people who have seen them floating up by the ceiling or anywhere else in the room. It's not uncommon too that people have also heard their loved ones in spirit talk to them, and some have carried on conversations with them.

Visions don't have to take place in the bedroom or when you're half asleep. One young man told me that he saw the apparition of his sister standing beside the gravestone at her burial. Other folks have seen them in different rooms of their home or even while driving their car. The key is to not get frightened. There is nothing scary in this situation. In fact, it's quite a beautiful sacred experience. Seeing a vision of your departed loved one is just their way of saying hello.

The next best thing to actually seeing a vision of your loved one is having them show up to say hello in your dream, which I discussed earlier when writing about dream visitations. This too is an after-death communication and a wonderful gift to receive.

Many people say they've heard their loved one's voice. In most cases, they heard their loved one in spirit calling their name. In these ADCs, people are not always physically hearing the voice with their ears but rather are hearing the voice in their mind (telepathically). Either way, it's a sign that your loved one is present.

In a similar way, lots of people claim to have felt the touch of their deceased loved one. Some say they felt it as a slight brush of their hand, a caressing touch on their neck, or even a kiss on the cheek. Others have felt an outright hug.

Possibly the most commonly reported after-death communication is when people feel the presence of their departed loved one. You don't see them or hear them, but you feel their presence—you just know they are in the room.

We do this with the living too. We might be lying on the couch with our eyes closed and listing to music through our iPod when all of a sudden we just know that someone has entered the room. Sometimes we know exactly who it is. Other times, we know someone is there, but we don't know who it is. Well, this is how it works when a spirit is present as well. We know they're there. We commonly know who it is. And we can feel their energy is near us.

There are several ADCs that are a little less direct than scents, visions, and touches. Our loved ones in spirit often use electricity and electrical appliances in order to get our attention and make their presence known.

About two weeks after my father passed, I was thinking about him while driving in my car and listening to the radio. Out of the blue, the radio began dialing from station to station as if someone were turning the knob. Yet the knob wasn't moving. The needle was moving across the dial, and I could hear the sound of the radio changing from station to station. This was before digital radios, so you really had to move the knob in order to move the needle.

I grabbed the knob to stop it, but it had no effect—the radio needle kept moving across the channels as if someone were controlling it. When it finally stopped about 30 seconds later, I suspected right away that it was my father saying hello. Even being a cynical skeptic at that time (before I began investigating the afterlife), I didn't know how I knew this—I just knew it was my father. And the radio never did it again, even though I owned that car for a couple more years.

It's easier for spirits to affect electricity and electronics like radios, televisions, clocks, and lights. Now I'll be the first person to say that a flickering light is often just a flickering light. But if you're at the dinner table with your family and you happen to be talking about your deceased loved one when the lights go off and then come back on again, that's a strong coincidence if the lights generally don't flicker in your house.

I know a man who lost his wife in her 40s. They had a daughter who was in her late teens at the time. One day, months after the woman passed, he and his daughter were arguing pretty loudly when his wife's favorite candlestick suddenly busted in half on the dining room table. It had never broken before and showed no signs of damage. It just broke in half in the middle of their shouting match. They stopped arguing immediately, taking it as a sign that the wife/mother wasn't pleased with their behavior.

The last thing I'll say about after-death communications is that the signals we get from our loved ones in spirit are always positive and meant to be joyful. If you interpret them as scary or negative in any way or you respond by feeling increased grief instead of comfort and reassurance, then they are going to stop letting you know that they are around. The purpose of ADCs is to make us feel good, not bad. So be grateful for the signs you get, and acknowledge them with joy by saying, "Hi, Mom. It's nice to hear from you. Thanks for stopping in today. Stick around for a while, and enjoy the party."

—∞—

Might my child's imaginary friend actually be a spirit?

It is actually quite common that children who interact with so-called imaginary friends are, in fact, playing with people in spirit. And these spirits can be anyone from a deceased relative (Grandpa, for instance) to the child's spirit guide or the neighbors' boy who passed and was visiting his parents next door. Imagine being a spirit who most humans cannot see, and then suddenly, some little boy who lives next to your parents notices you. If I were a spirit, I'd stick around to play with the child too.

My wife, Melissa, had an imaginary friend named Sally when she was a child. Everyone who knew Melissa knew about Sally. Today, Melissa is sure that Sally was a little girl in spirit. But of course, when Melissa was young, everyone thought Sally was a figment of her imagination.

Naturally, not all imaginary friends are spirits. The evidence is in the details. Start by asking your child questions about the friend to see if it might be someone you know.

I heard a story about a boy with an imaginary friend who turned out to be his grandfather. When his mother began questioning him about his friend, her son told her that it was her father. The mother was astonished because her father had passed before her son was born, and she (and her husband) hadn't shared anything about him with their son, believing he was too young to understand death. After further questioning of her son, he revealed things his grandfather told him that he could not have otherwise known, including a song the boy whistled that the grandfather often sang to his daughter when she was a girl. As you might expect, this promptly brought the woman to tears, and she no longer thought imaginary friends were only make-believe.

PART SEVEN

—꒳꒷—

QUESTIONS ABOUT READINGS WITH PSYCHIC MEDIUMS

What's the difference between a psychic and a medium?

Psychics (also known as intuitives) receive messages from Universal Energy, what some people call the quantum field, which includes your personal aura (energy). This ability is best used for guidance around life issues and direction.

The primary purpose of psychics, in my opinion, is to confirm to us what our own intuitions are telling us in order that we learn to trust our inner wisdom. If a psychic can help us do that, they've done a wonderful job.

Mediums (often called psychic mediums because they are both psychic and mediumistic) receive messages from spirits, including our deceased loved ones and our spirit guides, ascended masters, and angels. Their ability is best for spirit communication.

The primary purpose of mediums, in my opinion, is to provide evidence that our deceased loved ones are in spirit and are at peace in the afterlife. In this way, mediums help comfort and heal our grief, and they teach us to not fear death.

It is often said that all mediums are psychics (meaning that they have both abilities), but psychics are not mediums (meaning they have only psychic ability). This always seemed correct since psychic mediums are gifted to receive both psychic and mediumistic messages. However, in the last decade of my research, I've come to recognize that this discrepancy between psychics and psychic mediums isn't entirely accurate.

Due to the popularity of mediumship (spirit communication) in the last decade, I know dozens of psychics who have become excellent mediums as well. So evidence suggests that people who have psychic ability have a predisposition for mediumistic ability too. However, this doesn't mean that all psychics will be good at spirit communication. In fact, it's equally true that not all mediums are good at using their psychic ability either. Most people tend to be better at one or the other.

Think of psychics and mediums the same way you might think of lawyers and tax lawyers or general physicians and cardiologists. You can certainly go to your family lawyer about your taxes, and he'll be able to help you to a point. But you'd get better service regarding your taxes if you went to a tax lawyer. In the same manner, you could go see your general physician about your heart. But if she thinks you need more specialized knowledge, she's going to send you to a cardiologist.

Well, that's the difference between psychics and mediums. If you want information that comes from energy (guidance, direction, predictions), go to a psychic. If you're seeking spirit communication, go to a medium. It's that simple.

—ɷ—

What's the difference between a medium and a channeler?

Channelers (sometimes referred to as channels) are basically mediums with a specialty. They focus on communicating with spirit guides, ascended masters, and angels.

Traditionally, channelers channel messages from advanced spirits, usually to communicate spiritual wisdom about life and the afterlife. Many channelers work with the same higher-level spirit or a group of spirits their entire life. Jane Roberts, who channeled the *Seth* books, communicated with Seth, for instance. When communicating with a group of higher beings (often called nonphysical entities), channelers commonly refer to them by one name, such as Abraham, the Group, the Committee, or the Council. Paul Selig, who channeled *The Book of Knowing and Worth*, simply refers to his group as his guides.

If you're seeking to communicate with deceased loved ones in spirit, you'll want to use a medium. If you want to communicate with one or more advanced spirits for universal wisdom, you'll want to use a channeler.

—ɷ—

What are intuitives, empaths, and sensitives?

Intuitives, empaths, and sensitives are basically all the same, which is that they are people with a highly developed *psychic* ability. Some psychics use these alternative terms to label themselves because they feel the term more accurately describes their ability—such as an empath feels what other people are feeling. Others use these terms as a way to market themselves differently and stand out from the crowd, rather than just calling themselves a psychic.

—∿—

What are divination readers?

Divination readers use tools to give psychic readings and tell your future. The most common divination tool in the United States is the tarot deck. Other tools include tea leaves, runes, I Ching coins, crystals, crystal balls, scrying mirrors, pendulums, spirit boards or talking boards (Ouija board), and dowsing rods. Divination is typically not about spirit communication; therefore, mediums generally don't use them in readings of spirit communication. Divination is more about using tools for psychic readings and future predictions. While some divination readers depend on their tools of choice and use them strictly, intuitively gifted divination readers merely use their tools as a guide to get their intuition stimulated.

—∿—

Are psychic mediums legitimate?

Not all people claiming to be psychic mediums are legitimate. There are phonies, frauds, and scam artists just as in any practice, which is why I have tested hundreds of psychic mediums since 1999 to determine who is and who is not legitimate. But the answer is yes; there are many legitimately gifted mediums, including many whom I have not yet tested.

A legitimate medium is one who has a genuine ability to communicate with spirits. People sometimes refer to this ability as a gift. I've come to realize that we all have some degree of this ability that can be improved with training and experience. However, some people tend to be more naturally gifted than others, just like some people are more naturally gifted at singing, painting, or athletics.

I used to test psychic mediums for legitimacy alone but have come to test for other standards as well, such as ethics, integrity, professionalism, and responsibility in the delivery of messages. As a result, as the years have passed, it's become much more difficult to pass my test. So if a medium fails my test today, it doesn't mean he is a fake, necessarily; it might just mean that he doesn't deliver messages responsibly, which can be harmful and even dangerous to the person getting the reading.

If you are looking for a legitimate psychic medium, you'll want to check out my two websites: BestPsychicMediums.com and BestPsychicDirectory.com.

—◊—

How can I tell if a psychic medium is real or a fake?

Sadly, the average person is going to have a difficult time telling the difference between a legitimate medium and a fake. Phonies, frauds, and scam artists can be quite convincing. They can be good at deceiving people, especially people who are grieving or going through a desperate time in life as these people are often more susceptible to suggestion. Yet even legitimate mediums will show some of the signs I'll list below. So you can't assume that a medium is a fake just because they do. This is why it's difficult for the average person to spot a phony.

Here are the telltale signs to help you spot a phony or scam artist. You can usually spot one by looking for the following signs:

1. Fake psychic mediums and scam artists ask a lot of leading questions.

Some people call this a cold reading. For the most part, scam artists giving a cold reading are fishing around for clues so they can improve their guessing ratio when giving you messages. Yet not every medium who asks a lot of questions is a fake. There are many legitimate mediums who have developed poor habits of asking you a question about what they're seeing, hearing, or feeling instead of just presenting it as a statement.

"Who died in a car accident?" the medium might ask when what he should have said was "I have someone in spirit here who died in a car accident."

Or the medium might be given a message by the spirit to talk about a nurse, which will lead to information about the client's sister who is a nurse. But the medium might say, "Do you know someone who is a nurse?" or "Who is the nurse?"

What the medium should have said was "They are talking to me about a nurse. Does that make any sense to you?" If the client says yes, the medium can then get more information from the spirit that might lead to the next piece of information: "They are showing me that this nurse is a sibling of yours. I believe they're saying she's your sister."

So to sum up, phony mediums are known to ask a lot of questions. In fact, they have to ask questions in order to get anything right. Unfortunately, some legitimate mediums ask a lot of questions too, which is why it's so difficult for the average person to know if someone is real or not.

2. Fake psychic mediums and scam artists present vague, general messages rather than accurate evidence.

Spirit communication (mediumship) should always begin with messages that identify the spirit who is communicating with the psychic medium. What is their name? What are the circumstances of their passing? How old were they when they died? How long ago did they die? What was their physical appearance, and what were the characteristics of their personality? If the medium is unable to give you any identifying evidence of this type, that's a red flag that they might be a fake. Otherwise, it's merely a sign that the medium is inexperienced or poorly gifted.

3. Fake psychic mediums and scam artists claim that you are cursed.

You should never give money to any psychic or medium who promises to remove a curse or spell for a fee. There is never any curse or spell, and this is the most common scam in this field. These criminals are merely using fear to manipulate people. And scam artists who promise to remove a curse for a fee have been known to charge (and get) thousands, even tens of thousands, of dollars from people by using this common scam.

Sometimes they'll say that they can remove the curse for you—for a fee. They might tell you that they can remove the curse in one session or tell you it will take multiple sessions to remove it (and you have to pay them each session). Sometimes they'll say you have to purchase a high-priced crystal (or some other object) in order to remove the curse—and buy it from them, of course. These are typical scams that take place all the time.

Since the scam artist pretending to be a legitimate medium (or psychic) usually knows a lot about the client by this point in their relationship (because she's encouraged a codependent relationship), she likely knows how much money the client has in the bank. And lo and behold, she'll tell the client that it will cost approximately that same amount to remove the curse. Wow, what a coincidence!

"But don't worry," the psychic will say, "because once this curse is removed, you'll have all sorts of new money coming your way." Once they've instilled fear in the client, they motivate them further by promising how wonderful the client's life will be once the curse is gone.

I've heard tragic stories where people have lost $12,000 to $27,000 due to this scam. It's not the amount that makes these scams especially tragic; it's that the amount is often the person's entire life savings. And even if the attorney general's office catches these scam artists and puts them in jail, the victims of these psychic scams rarely ever get their money back.

4. Fake psychic mediums and scam artists ask you for personal information like your social security number, driver's license number, bank account numbers, and passwords.

Never give out your social security number, driver's license number, bank account numbers, or passwords to a psychic medium. If one asks you for this information, it's a strong sign that something suspicious is up. Hang up, and report them to your state attorney general's office.

—⚮—

What is a spirit artist?

A spirit artist is a medium who draws portraits of the spirits they see. Essentially, we're talking about a medium who is also an artist since they have the ability to draw a picture of the person in spirit with whom they are communicating.

Usually, the spirit artist gives you a reading verbally at the same time that they are drawing this visual rendering of your deceased loved one. It's quite an amazing experience because it takes the reading of spirit communication—which is usually intangible evidence—and turns it into tangible evidence, something you can hold in your hands and show other people (the portrait).

I'll never forget the first time I had a spirit drawing done. The spirit artist drew my grandmother. She got my grandmother's hair, chin, eyes, and even her typical clothing style correct. In most cases, there is going to be one to three key features that clearly identify that the spirit artist has connected with your loved one. There might be some slight variation from what you remember of your loved one's appearance, but this happens even when artists draw people who are alive and standing right in front of them.

My second session with a spirit artist was done over the phone. I had a fantastic reading where my great-great-grandfather came through. The spirit artist told me my great-great-grandfather was wearing a Civil War uniform and had a cleft chin, deep-set eyes, and long hair. This all sounded accurate as I had seen a photograph of him years prior, and I knew the photograph was of him in his Civil War uniform.

After the phone session, the spirit artist mailed my spirit drawing to my post office box. At the same time, I called my mother and asked her to mail me the only photo that existed of my great-great-grandfather, which she had to get from my aunt. When the photograph and the spirit drawing both arrived, I was astonished to see how alike they were. The only slight difference between them was that my great-great-grandfather appeared a little older to the medium than he was when the photo was taken. But looking at the two photos side by side, it was unmistakable that it was the same person.

To see this spirit drawing beside the photo of my great-great-grandfather, visit this page online: http://www.bestpsychicmediums.com/Rita-Article.htm.

—ɷ—

Can I choose which loved ones in spirit come through in my reading?

You can pray to the loved ones in spirit whom you'd like to show up for your reading and request that they be there, but there are never any guarantees. Psychic mediums are like telephones to the spirit world without a dial. They can pick up the phone and see who is there, but they can't dial directly to any one spirit. In most cases, the person with whom you wish to communicate will show up to the reading, but it's never guaranteed.

—ɷ—

I had a reading with a psychic medium, but my deceased loved one didn't come through. What does this mean?

As mentioned, mediums cannot summon whatever spirit they choose, so they have no control over who shows up for a reading. But 95 percent of the time, at least, the loved one with whom you hope to communicate will come through. So what does it mean for that small percentage of readings where they don't show up? This is one of those situations where there is more than one possible reason.

If you have never been to a medium before and you might never go again, spirits only have this single opportunity to communicate with you. Consequently, those in spirit, including your spirit guides, are going to get the most important messages through first—from the most important people.

For example, even though you might want to communicate with your recently deceased mother, it might be more important that your friend comes through to tell you he doesn't blame you for the car accident that killed him when you were teenagers, especially if you were driving. Or it might be more important that your stepfather comes through to request your forgiveness for being abusive or forgive you for something you did or said before he passed. Or it might even be more important that your neighbor's grandmother comes through asking you to tell her daughter (your neighbor) that her grandmother is alive in spirit.

Not that we have any choice, but we have to trust that spirit knows what's most imperative. Even though you might prefer to hear from your recently deceased mother more than your high school friend, your friend's message might be more important for your peace of mind or spiritual growth.

In the same way, while some people aren't pleased about paying for a reading where their neighbor, friend, or relative gets a message, a spirit might know that those people are never going to get a reading, so they employ you as their messenger to deliver an important message. Feel good about this opportunity to help another, and know that you can always get another reading. What the spirit is saying in this situation is that they know that you are strong enough to work through your grief if your reading is briefly cut short for another's benefit, or they know that you'll be back for another reading in the future.

It's a rare occurrence when you get more messages for another than you get for yourself. This generally only happens at medium demonstrations (live events) when the medium is only giving 10-minute readings to audience members. Even then, this doesn't happen frequently.

This is one reason I recommend people get a one-hour reading versus a half-hour reading. Obviously, if you have more time, it's more likely that you'll hear from the person that you want because the most important messages can come first and there'll still be time for the loved one you're seeking to come through if he or she didn't show up immediately.

Some people believe that our loved ones in spirit need time to reintegrate to the afterlife before they'll show up to a reading, especially in the case of suicide, murder, or sudden death. Yet I've witnessed readings where people who have taken their own life, been murdered, or died suddenly showed up during a reading just hours or days after their death.

Some mediums say it's common that our loved ones who have been in spirit for a longer time help bring through those who have recently passed. Sometimes we might not even know about this assistance during a reading, but it does happen. But don't worry if no one else in your family has passed prior to your loved one in spirit as there's always distant relatives, spirit guides, and spirits this person knew before they were born to greet them back home into the spirit world and help them communicate with their surviving loved ones here on the earth plane.

I don't actually believe time has anything to do with one spirit helping another spirit to communicate with us humans. I believe that some spirits are just better at communicating with us than others. So when a grandfather helps his recently deceased grandson communicate with the boy's mother, it might not be because the grandfather has been in spirit longer. It's more likely that the grandfather is just better at this type of communication. He probably helps people who have been in spirit *longer* than him as well.

It's fairly rare that the loved one you most want to hear from doesn't show up at your reading, so there is always a good reason for it when it happens. Sometimes it has more to do with what's going on with you than it does them. Your physical and mental state of mind can affect your reading. I know a woman who called a medium once in order to make a reading appointment. When the medium answered the phone, her deceased mother immediately made contact and began giving the medium messages. The connection was strong, and the messages were loud and clear. However, the medium didn't have time to give the reading at that moment, so they made the appointment for the next day.

The woman was so nervous about her reading that she drank a bottle of wine that evening. The next day, when she showed up at the reading with a hangover, the medium was negatively affected by the woman's depleted energy. He said that while the woman's mother was definitely coming through, the connection was foggy and faint—a distinct contrast from the day before. As a result, the reading was less than satisfying for the woman, and she was entirely responsible for it. It had absolutely nothing to do with her mother and everything to do with her own state of mind.

Spirit communication through a medium is a three-way conversation. All three parties—the sitter, the medium, and the spirit—affect the reading. If the sitter (client) or the medium arrives with their energy low, the reading won't be as good as when everyone's energy is high.

Be conscious to avoid negatively affecting your energy prior to a reading due to alcohol, drugs, stress, an argument, lack of sleep, too much exercise, or too many concerns weighing on your mind. You're expected to be nervous if this is your first reading, but nervous energy isn't necessarily low energy unless you try to suppress it with drugs or alcohol. Just allow your nervousness to play out as enthusiasm, and be optimistic and playful during the reading. The spirit-to-medium connection will likely be better as a result.

At the same time, don't book a reading if your grief is such that you are in a desperate state of mind. Desperation is a lower-energy emotion. If you're feeling fraught with despair or overly anxious about contacting your departed loved one, it might be best to see a grief counselor first. If your loved ones in spirit don't think you can manage the messages in a healthy manner, they might choose to not come through for your sake. Plus it can be really distracting for a medium if you're sobbing uncontrollably while she's trying to communicate with your loved ones. This can disrupt the medium from giving her best reading because she's so concerned about you.

Having covered all these bases, it's also true that mediums have bad days, just like the rest of us. They too get stressed, depressed, and tired. If the medium was able to get clear messages from one or two relatives but not from the person in spirit whom you wanted, then this is probably not the issue. But if none of the messages seemed accurate or there were a few minor hits but a lot more misses, it's possible that the medium was having an off day.

In this case, always let the medium know early in the reading that the messages are not making sense. This way, the medium can stop the reading and book it for another day. Don't wait until the reading is over before you say something. That's not fair to the medium, and it's not fair to you.

Always keep in mind that regardless of what happens or doesn't happen at your reading, there will be future opportunities for other readings. Too many people put so much pressure on the reading as if they'll never get another chance to connect with their loved ones. Yet this just isn't true.

There will be other chances. If you want to connect with your loved one in spirit, you'll have another opportunity if it's a priority in your life. And don't forget that you are always connected to your loved ones. You don't need a medium present in order to communicate with them. Sometimes you just need to trust in your own ability to recognize the signs that are all around you. Some people call this faith. If you have faith and a little patience, you'll eventually connect with your loved one in spirit in some way—through a medium, in a dream, via an after-death communication (ADC), maybe even during meditation.

—⁓—

Can I prevent certain people in spirit from coming through in my reading?

You can certainly ask people in spirit (before a reading) to not show up at your reading. But no, you really can't prevent spirits from showing up.

On more than one occasion, I've witnessed an ex-husband's mother show up hoping her former daughter-in-law (who was getting the reading) would pass a message on to the spirit's son. I've even seen departed relatives of a neighbor arrive at the reading hoping the person getting the reading would share a message with the spirit's relative (the neighbor). This doesn't happen frequently, but it does happen more often than you might expect.

Another typical yet unwanted occurrence at a reading is when an abusive parent, relative, or spouse (now in spirit) shows up pleading for forgiveness when the person getting the reading wants nothing to do with him or her. These are difficult situations for everyone involved. And it's during cases like these when you realize that spirit communication isn't all about you.

Even though you paid for the reading, spirit communication also holds benefits for those in spirit. So if someone you know in spirit needs to tell you that they are sorry for something they did or said to you, it might be equally important for you to hear it, even if you don't think you want to hear it. You aren't required to forgive them, of course. But it can be healing to know that they are remorseful for their actions.

The best thing to do when a spirit who you don't want there shows up at your reading is to simply allow their message to come through. Let their message be conveyed so that the reading can move on to another spirit. From my experience witnessing this type of situation in numerous medium demonstrations (readings from a stage in a live arena), if you waste time telling the medium that you don't want to hear from that spirit, it's unlikely to change anything and will only waste time. Some people in spirit will continue to distract the medium until they get their message through.

So let what needs to be said come through, and then move forward. You might actually discover that the message you get is exactly what you need to hear. And don't forget, you get to talk back and say whatever you want to say to them as well. That's one of the greatest benefits of spirit communication—it's a conversation, not a monologue. You can talk right out loud to the person in spirit, and they'll hear everything you have to say. Even if you wait until after the reading when you're home alone, that spirit will still hear what you have to say. So go ahead, and get what you're feeling off your chest. Sometimes that's what's required before any healing can take place.

—∿∿—

How long should I wait after someone has passed before getting a reading with a psychic medium?

After all my investigations into the afterlife, I've concluded that there is no proper time to wait before getting a reading, despite what some mediums might tell you. If you want a reading, go ahead and get one regardless of how much time has passed since the person died.

The most common reason some people say you should wait weeks or months after a person has died is because those people believe it takes time for the newly deceased to acclimate to their new existence as spirits. My investigation into life after death suggests otherwise. There is no concept of time in the afterlife, so there is no need for a waiting period, at least not for the reasons these people argue. The only reason some people believe that there is a transition period when returning home to the spirit world is because we, as humans, can only think linearly—that is, we can't imagine what it's like without time.

I do believe in a transitionary phase from our physical death to our spiritual return, but not in terms of time. This transition can happen in a heartbeat, even though it might be quite complex for the person in spirit. So I'm not suggesting that there isn't a transitionary phase.

I'm merely saying that it doesn't take any time. It can happen in an instant.

I have witnessed readings where people who died that very same day came through. In some of these cases, the sitters having the reading didn't even know the person had passed. In other readings, it had only been a few days or a couple of weeks. In all cases, the people in spirit came through loud and clear as well as happy, healthy, and at peace. After all, a spirit knows no other state of being other than happy, healthy, and at peace. This is true even for people who have taken their own lives, which is a circumstance that some people believe requires extra time to acclimate once the deceased has crossed over to the other side. But when there's no time, there's no acclimation period in the way that we commonly imagine. Again, everything is happening instantaneously.

Having said this, while I've seen no need for waiting for the sake of our loved ones in spirit, I do feel it's occasionally healthy to wait to get a reading for the sitter's sake. It is traumatic losing a loved one. Grief hits us on many levels, many of which we are unaware. It often requires weeks, months, or sometimes years for some people to be ready for a reading with a medium. I personally recommend that people wait a few weeks, at least. Otherwise, your state of bereavement might be such that you are feeling desperate and hopeless, which are not good emotional states for a healthy mediumistic reading.

When you are finally able to talk about your late loved one without falling into a fit of sobbing hysteria, it's probably safe to say that you've healed enough to get a reading. You'll likely cry during your reading, which is expected and normal. But the key is that you want the reading to be healing, not distressing. Most psychic mediums are not therapists or counselors, so they are not equipped to help frantic, inconsolable clients who are emotionally distraught by the mere thought of connecting with their loved ones in the hereafter.

Worse, some mediums can misinterpret messages that might add to a bereaved person's fearful concerns rather than comfort them. Hence, it's important that you be mentally stable enough to be able to accept only those messages that make sense and discard any messages that seem in error. Sadly, those who are desperate for a connection to the recently departed tend to accept everything as true, and that's simply not healthy. It's also not reality. Mediums misinterpret messages at times.

In the end, I don't believe you have to wait for a reading for your departed loved one's sake, but you might want to wait for a reading for your sake. You want to be sure that you are emotionally stable enough to be discerning with the messages that you get. When you feel you are ready at this level, that's the best time to get a reading.

—∿—

What should I expect in my reading with a psychic medium?

At the beginning of your reading, most mediums will begin with some small talk, a few instructions of what you should or should not do (e.g., only tell them if you understand or don't understand a message, but don't feed them information), and a quick rundown of how they work. Some might say a brief prayer or statement of intention. Then they will usually jump into the reading.

There might be a brief pause as the medium connects with the spirits who are present. In most cases, one spirit will begin the communication, and the medium will tell you a few details in order to identify who it is. It will usually go something like this (this would be a really good reading):

"I have a male in his midthirties who has been in spirit only about two or three years, definitely less than five years. He has dark hair and is of medium build, though he's rather tall, maybe about six feet in height. He's telling me that he died on the job. He was a police officer. I'm feeling a blow to the head, like he died due to striking his head on something. It feels like he was in a car accident. I'm getting that he was chasing someone in his police car and hit a tree. He says he died instantly upon impact—no suffering. Does any of this make sense to you?"

At this point, you say yes or no. The medium will then tell you more information about this police officer and perhaps describe his personality, his hobbies, and his position in the family (middle child, for example).

Another example of a reading might go like this:

"I'm getting the name Sal or Salvador. He liked to play soccer. No, he's correcting me. He loved to play soccer. It was his favorite pastime. He's making me feel like he hurt his knee at some point. Either he hurt his knee playing soccer, or his knee bothered him when he played soccer. And he wasn't married, but he's showing me a ring—it looks like an engagement ring, so he was either engaged or he was about to ask someone to marry him. Yes, he's telling me that he had bought the ring but hadn't asked her to marry him yet. That seems to be a regret of his—that he never got to marry his sweetheart. Oh, he's telling me that you are his sweetheart. You are the woman he planned to marry but never got to ask for your hand in marriage and give you the ring. Is this correct?"

The medium might ask for some confirmation that she's on the right track and then continue.

"Sal's larger than life. He's showing me that he's animated when he talks and the kind of guy who likes to put his arm around people and give them a one-armed hug. He's very affectionate. He really loved his family and his friends. He has a big heart. I'm getting that he was the oldest of maybe five kids. He's showing me two girls and three boys. And he's showing me the number 1, which usually means to me that he was the firstborn.

"Sal is now letting me know that his father met him when he crossed over, so his father is in spirit. And his mother is still alive. She is taking his passing very hard. She's still having a difficult time with it. He wants to be sure you tell her he acknowledges her and that he's okay. I'm getting that you aren't in contact with her often. But if there is a way that you can get that message to her, maybe through one of the other siblings, it would be helpful to her."

The typical reading goes something like that. This, of course, would be a reading with a highly gifted, well-trained, and experienced medium. The less gifted, less trained, and less experienced would probably get some of these messages but with less detail. Still, even if you only got half this detail in a reading, it would still be quite healing.

You never know how long any medium might spend on one spirit. She might spend the entire reading on one spirit, or she might get messages from three, four, or five spirits. Since every reading is limited by time, the more spirits that come through, the less detail you'll get from each person in spirit. You can certainly let the medium know ahead of time what you prefer. You might tell her that if your father comes through, you'd prefer she stay with your father until he's said all that he has to say before moving on to another person in spirit.

Mediums with less training and experience have less control over their readings. So a reading at this lower level of ability might fire off random messages from several spirits, often confusing which spirit is delivering what message. In one of the best readings I ever had, the medium told the spirits in attendance to line up so she could read them one at a time. But many mediums don't realize they can do that, so they tend to tell you what they're getting as they get it as if a group of people in spirit are all yelling messages at the same time, and the medium just tells you what he's hearing.

With the best mediums, once they have identified the physical characteristics of the person in spirit, their personality, their cause of death, their hobbies and interests, their relationships, and the memories they had with you, they usually end with some messages of love, forgiveness, or advice. They might tell you how much they love you, how proud they are of you, or how they are watching over you or encourage you to do something that will be positive in your life.

At some point, when the reading is coming to a close, the medium might allow you the remaining few minutes to ask questions. Once your allotted time is over, the reading comes to an end.

—∞—

What is "evidential" mediumship?

The reading I just described above follows the structure of an evidential reading with a medium.

An evidential mediumistic reading usually begins with messages that give you evidence that your loved one in spirit is truly communicating with the medium. The reading with the medium generally starts with a presentation of physical evidence, such as her appearance, cause of death, age, and sex. The messages then describe your loved one's personality, including what she liked and disliked, identifying speech patterns, and unique characteristics about her that serve as evidence that it is truly her who is coming through in the reading. The psychic medium will likely even use words or phrases that your loved one would typically use. Then there will be some messages to describe your loved one's history growing up, her family situation, her marital status, and if she has had any children or pets.

The purpose of evidential mediumship is to help you overcome any skepticism you might have about spirit communication. Evidential messages are the messages that people often describe as follows: "The medium knew things about her that he could never have known unless he was in direct contact with her." When you're getting a reading from a medium who is a stranger to you and knows nothing about you—which I recommend—then this evidence is even more powerful. Then after all the evidential messages have been delivered, the medium will present the messages that are meaningful and loving, though nonevidential.

—⦚—

Is there a difference between an American and a British psychic medium?

A medium is a medium regardless of where in the world they live. But most British mediums are trained to give evidence-based readings, as described above, which provide evidence that the messages the medium is giving you are legitimate. This isn't to say there aren't psychic mediums in England who don't practice evidential mediumship, but I've found most British mediums tend to follow a formula that gives evidence first and then other messages and guidance second.

You never really know what you're going to get with mediums from the United States unless they have been trained in evidential mediumship. If they've been trained at a Spiritualist church by another evidential medium or by teachers at the Arthur Findlay College in England, they are likely trained in evidential spirit communication.

I've also noticed that mediums from the United States (including evidential mediums) tend to read at a faster pace than most British mediums, which I personally prefer. The slower, formulaic pace of British mediumship leaves me slightly impatient. This is probably indicative of our fast-paced society in the United States, at least in Massachusetts, where I grew up. Nonetheless, I'm not the only person to have commented on the slow, relaxed style of British mediumship, which some people like better because it's easier to follow.

—∞—

Are evidence-focused mediums better than other mediums?

Everyone has their preferences when it comes to psychic mediums. It's impossible to say which style of reading is better. It's more about which style is better for you.

From my perspective, however, I like evidential spirit communication because it gives us evidence that the messages are really coming from our loved ones in spirit. The way my mind works, if the medium has given me extraordinary evidence that they could not have possibly known without getting it from my deceased loved one, then it helps me to believe the other nonevidential messages. But without the evidential messages, there's really no way to know if anything the medium is saying is true. So because I always begin with skepticism first, I prefer the evidence before I feel confident believing in the nonspecific messages.

—∞—

Are there schools for psychic mediums?

Mediumship (spirit communication) isn't being taught at Stanford, Yale, or Harvard, at least not yet. However, the Arthur Findlay

College in Stansted, England, focuses its curriculum on psychic and mediumistic development. And more and more psychics and mediums are traveling there for a week or two at a time.

Does a week or two at the Arthur Findlay College make an excellent medium? No, not in itself, but it shows that the medium who goes there is doing what she can to improve her ability. So it's a sign that she is serious about improving her ability if that medium has made the investment in herself, which isn't just the tuition but also the travel expenses and time required.

Second, there are dozens of mediums who offer instruction for mediumistic development. Most of these classes are for beginners, but a few offer more advanced development classes. Of course, it's important to note that just because someone is a good medium doesn't necessarily mean they are a good teacher. While some of these instructors are surely talented teachers too, some mediums are not.

I'm impressed when a medium invests in a program of some sort in order to improve his or her ability. To me, it's evidence that this medium is doing what he can to give better readings. But then it's also important to me to know who is behind the organization offering the program and/or who is teaching it. In my mind, if it's a reputable organization and a reputable teacher to boot, it adds credibility to that psychic medium's résumé. Yet on the other hand, when I see a medium who has trained with a teacher who I know needs training herself, that reflects poorly upon my first impression of that medium.

—ɷ—

Are certified psychic mediums better?

Some psychic mediums present themselves as "certified" by some person or organization. This is because some of the classes being offered give certifications to the students who complete the class. However, certifications of this type don't hold a lot of weight in my opinion because there are no governing bureaus accrediting these "classes" or "instructors," and therefore, there is no one evaluating the class or holding the instructors accountable.

Basically, in these cases, the certification means the person passed that class, though we (the consumer) have no idea what requirements exist in order to pass the class or how difficult (and thorough) the class was in the first place. It's possible that every student passes just by paying the fee and showing up.

As of the time of this writing, there are no certifications for mediums that indicate that a "certified medium" is the cream of the crop. Nonetheless, I like to see both psychics and mediums being trained to improve their ability, so any certification at least indicates they are taking classes or courses to improve their readings rather than floundering on their own without instruction. On the other hand, since it's also possible that underqualified teachers are training these mediums poorly or even improperly, certifications hold little weight in my mind when choosing a medium for my websites or myself.

—ɷ—

Is there a code of ethics for psychic mediums?

No, there is no code of ethics that governs all psychics or mediums and no board or governing agency that oversees psychics and mediums. There are laws that protect the public against fraud, which are usually governed by the state attorney general's office, but these can differ from state to state.

Don't be fooled by websites that have appointed themselves as a governing agency, association, or bureau in the psychic or medium field. There are no such organizations acting on behalf of the government or any consumer group, regardless of how official their website looks.

In most cases, such websites that present themselves with the image that they are a governing or overseeing board in this field are merely promotional venues for an individual psychic or medium to advertise themselves. The evidence of this is that you'll notice one psychic or medium (often the owner of the site) is posted all over the site in order to promote his or her reading services. It fools a lot of people, which is why they do it. But now it won't fool you.

—⚸—

Are famous mediums better than nonfamous mediums?

Famous psychic mediums usually become famous because they are good in the first place (though not always). And they typically get a lot more experience once they are famous, which consequently makes them better than they were before they got famous. And if they are giving readings on television or in front of thousands of people at live events, then they are getting a lot of feedback from people. This holds them accountable to be the best they can be as mediums.

Aside from this, however, the answer is no, famous mediums are not necessarily better than nonfamous mediums.

This is really a question of common sense. We all know celebrities who are nasty people. Just because they are famous doesn't make them nicer people. Criminals have even become famous, but we wouldn't want to invite them for a sleepover. And the same is true for famous mediums. There are nice ones, mean ones, honest ones, dishonest ones, highly gifted ones, and poorly gifted ones. Just because they're on TV or have written a best-selling book doesn't make them any better or worse than any other medium.

There will always be people on the planet who feel that they absolutely must get a reading with a famed TV medium—even though the reading costs more than they can afford. These people assume the medium is the best because she's on television. The truth is that being a great psychic medium is not the first criterion for getting your own TV show. Being entertaining is actually the first criterion.

Still, there are mediums whose reputations live up to their fame. I've watched and analyzed medium John Edward giving readings during a live event in Boston and found him to be absolutely extraordinary. George Anderson, another well-known medium who used to be on TV more in my early years of investigating the afterlife, seems to live up to his reputation as well. And I saw James Van Praagh give live medium demonstrations that absolutely blew my mind. He gave one of the best readings I've ever seen from a medium the very first time I saw him demonstrate.

These three famous mediums are highly gifted, and their abilities have benefited a great deal from their years of giving thousands of readings. But I've also tested mediums who are virtually unknown who are also impressive. This is not to take away from John, George, or James. I admire them as mediums and as trailblazers who have paved the way for other mediums to do what they do. But I have no doubt that they would all agree with me when I say that there are lesser-known mediums with remarkable ability, integrity, and professionalism who likely charge a lot less and are much more accessible. And I say this only so you don't feel that you must get a reading from a famous medium in order to get a great reading. It truly isn't necessary.

Since I've mentioned John, George, and James, I should also mention that they each have a handful of books on mediumship and the afterlife that everyone interested in these subjects should read. My favorite John Edward book is still his first, titled *One Last Time*. Likewise, my favorite James Van Praagh book is still his first, titled *Talking To Heaven*. And there's a book written about George Anderson that anyone with remaining skepticism should read. It's titled *We Don't Die* by Joel Martin and Patricia Romanowski.

—⁊⁊⁊—

How much does a good reading with a psychic medium cost?

The reality is that you can get a good reading for $25 to $65 an hour. But the likelihood that you'll get an extraordinary reading with a highly gifted, well-experienced, and properly trained medium in this range is low. As mediums grow in ability, often, so does their fee, at least with most of them.

So top mediums will generally cost between $100 and $350 for a one-hour reading. That's the going rate as I write this. As for mediums who are famous in various degrees (authors or TV personalities), their rates can average from $300 to over $1,000 for a one-hour reading.

It's really just a matter of supply and demand. As a medium grows in ability, their reputation tends to grow too, which usually results in their audience growing. When this happens, there tends to be more demands on their time as well. The result is that their fee tends to increase, which can empower them to reach even more people with their work and message (that we survive death).

—⁓—

What's the purpose of psychic medium readings?

The purpose of readings with mediums is to communicate with our deceased loved ones, which helps comfort and heal our grief. It gives us evidence that our deceased loved ones still exist, only they now exist in spirit. It teaches us that the departed are still with us and watching over us. And it informs us about the afterlife.

Spirit communication through a medium also teaches us that we survive death. Once a person develops a "knowing" that life after death is real, their entire perspective, and therefore their entire life, changes in positive ways. Many of our psychological problems are based on our fear of death. And since the mind-body connection is so powerful, losing this fear can help us physically as well as psychologically.

Mediumistic readings also show us that there is more to life and death than most people realize—much more than we can perceive using our five senses. This inspires us to seek more information, to investigate the truth, and to explore new experiences that lead us to deeper understandings of where we come from and where we are going. And these are just some of the many benefits we gain from readings with mediums.

—✺—

My reading was terrible! Was I scammed?

So you had a lousy reading, and now you're wondering if the medium is a scam artist. There are multiple facets to this answer because it's rarely so cut-and-dry. If your reading with a medium had absolutely no hits (nothing rang true for you), it's possible that the medium is a fraud. It's also possible that the medium is legitimate but not very good (poor natural ability or poorly trained, if trained at all) or that she was having a bad day.

As discussed earlier in this book, scam artists are usually looking for more than the mere profit they can make from the reading fee alone. What they really want is to find an impressionable client who comes to rely upon them after several readings, at which point they will tell her that she has a curse on her. They'll say that this curse is blocking her from success in her career, relationships, health, or all of the above. And it's at this point when the scam artist tells the client that they can remove the curse for a fee.

I'm sure there are some phony psychics and mediums who are satisfied with just giving readings and not going for the big rip-off. But this is more difficult with mediums since spirit communication requires evidential messages. So if you had a lousy reading with a medium but you did get some messages that were strong hits, it's quite likely that you weren't scammed. Chances are you just got a bad reading. Either you chose a medium who is poorly gifted, or you chose a highly gifted medium who simply had a bad day. There is also one other possibility.

It's also possible that you were let down more by your expectations than by the medium's reading ability. Some people are looking to hear from one—and only one—person in spirit, so no matter who else comes through and no matter how accurate the messages might be from those other spirits, that client is going to be unsatisfied with the reading because he didn't get the spirit he wanted.

Other people are let down by their own expectations because they expect too many details. Most mediums are not going to give you full names, exact addresses, or dates with the month, day, and year or be spot-on accurate with every message. If you're expecting the evidence to be that detailed or the spirit communication to be as clear as two people talking on the telephone, you're likely going to be disappointed. But this isn't indicative of a scam. You just expected more than is typical for spirit communication with a medium or maybe even more than is possible.

Your skepticism can also be a factor. Sometimes a client's closed-minded skepticism gets in his way, and he's unable to recognize a good reading when he gets one. I was this way in the first two years of my investigation. After my father passed in 1997, I saw lots of psychics and thought every one of them to be a fraud. Chances are I was just too cynical and closed-minded to accept any messages that weren't evidence-based. That doesn't mean the psychics weren't good. It just means that I wasn't ready to accept their vague generalities without strong evidence. What I needed was a reading with an evidential medium, which I finally got in 1999. But from 1997 to 1999, I didn't even know what a medium was—as most people didn't back then—so I mistakenly went to psychics (versus mediums) looking for evidential messages from spirits.

If your reading was disappointing yet you chose a reputable medium based on the testimonials of other people (and you had realistic expectations), the probability is that you weren't scammed. The probability is that you merely got a poor reading. I recommend that you contact the medium and let him know about your dissatisfaction.

Ask him if he thinks the reading went okay or if it's possible that he was having an off day. Of course, be gentle in your wording since most psychic mediums are very sensitive. You don't want to be antagonistic or mean as aggressiveness only invites defensiveness. If you are gentle in your complaint, many mediums are honest enough to admit if they were having a bad day and will possibly offer you a second reading at no extra charge.

If the medium disagrees that it was a bad reading, she might tell you that it was an excellent reading and that your skepticism blocked you from recognizing it. If this is the case, listen to the recording again, or look over your notes to see if you might have missed some strong evidence. Were some messages accurate even if most were not? Was there any information conveyed that the medium could not possibly have known without some gifted ability? If this is the case, your reading might have fallen short in your opinion, but it doesn't mean you were scammed. It just means that you chose a medium who needs training, needs more experience, or maybe had a bad day.

The last possibility I'll cover here is what's called "psychic amnesia." Many people who get a reading become filled with anxiety and can't think clearly when the medium gives them a message. This is called psychic amnesia because you forget the details of your life all of a sudden. Some people have forgotten their siblings' names. Others have forgotten what their grandfather did for a living or that their mother lost a child while giving birth (a child who is technically their sibling).

If the medium gave you some messages that were compelling hits and other hits were missed by you because of psychic amnesia, the reading might have been better than you realized. While I don't generally recommend that people share their readings with others, this might be one exception for doing so. If you share your reading with a parent or sibling who has a good memory, that person might recognize some messages the medium gave you that you thought were in error. Now when you add up the compelling hits that you recognized along with these "psychic amnesia" hits that you originally missed, you might realize that the reading was actually pretty good (at the very least not the work of a scam artist).

I believe that every reading is a stepping-stone in our journey of spiritual growth. Even my worst readings over the years—and I've had many—taught me something valuable about spirit communication and spirituality. At a minimum, they taught me to appreciate the better readings. So not all is lost when you get a bad reading. After all, if you get another reading in the future—and I recommend that you do—you'll be much more careful about which medium you choose, and now you have at least one reading to help you evaluate the next one.

—⁓—

I was given predictions about my future during my reading. Are predictions accurate?

Because this book is about the afterlife, I'm going to concentrate this answer on predictions given by our deceased loved ones during readings with mediums. I've discussed predictions by psychics on my websites, so you can find that answer there.

I'm not a big fan of predictions because I've seen too many misinterpreted by mediums, thereby causing confusion and chaos in people's lives. When I get a prediction from a loved one in spirit during a reading with a medium, I don't give it a lot of weight. Instead, I consider it while matching it with what my own intuition is telling me. And if the prediction is quite serious yet my intuition isn't telling me anything, I'll file that prediction in the back of my mind to see if any other signs that have a similar message come into my life.

I'm much more likely to trust my own intuition and the signs I get from the Universe, such as divine messengers or divine coincidences. I use the word 'divine' to indicate that my soul and spirit guides have put these messengers and coincidences in front of me for guidance.

For example, I once had a reading where a loved one in spirit mentioned something about getting my pickup truck fixed. I hadn't had any mechanical work done, so I just kept the prediction in mind. The following week, I kept bumping into a guy in town who drove the same pickup truck as me (that's all we had in common). I rarely saw him, but in that one week, I saw him four times. So the fourth time we crossed paths, I chatted with him and asked him how his truck was running. He told me about a recall on the truck that he recently had fixed, which I didn't know about. So I made sure to get the recalled part replaced, and I haven't seen the man since.

I have been told many predictions over the years that did not come to fruition, which is why I'm not a big fan of predictions. Too many people think future predictions are set in stone when, in reality, they are merely snapshots of what "might" happen, not what "will" happen. Because we have free will, we each have the power to change what psychic mediums (and people in spirit) see in our future. In fact, you could hang up the phone after a reading and instantly alter the prediction that was made in that reading simply by making an alternate choice.

Just think of a prediction as a photograph taken through the windshield of your car. This photo indicates the direction your car is heading, but it doesn't take into account that you might make a right or left turn along the way. Free will is our ability to make right and left turns before we reach the destination in the photograph. Make one turn, and suddenly, the prediction (the photo) changes.

—⋙—

What are the most common messages that come from loved ones in spirit in a reading with a psychic medium?

Some of the more common messages from people in spirit during a reading with a psychic medium are as follows:

1. *"I'm okay."* Immediately following their passing, people in spirit want their loved ones to know that they are okay—they are happy, healthy, and alive. Mainly, they want us to know that they survived death; that is, they did not disappear but rather still exist, only now in spirit form versus physical form.

2. *"My suffering ended the second I died."* Many people worry that their loved ones continue to suffer from their illness, injuries, or mental

anguish after death. Therefore, one of the most common messages from people in spirit is that their suffering ended the moment they left their bodies. Once in spirit, they were free from all human and physical suffering.

3. *"I am closer to you now than I ever was before."* People in spirit commonly convey through mediums that they can see, hear, and even read their surviving loved one's thoughts. Consequently, our loved ones in spirit know more about what's going on with us physically, emotionally, and spiritually and therefore feel closer to us than when they were living in their physical bodies.

4. *"I'm watching over you."* As an expansion of the prior message, our loved ones in spirit commonly want us to know that they are watching over us from the spirit world and guiding us when appropriate and possible. This doesn't mean, however, that they are constantly hovering over us at every second, but they check in on us regularly and come to our side whenever we think of them.

In this way, they always know what is going on in our lives (our triumphs and disappointments). They are watching when we graduate from college, become a parent, get a new job, and even when we become ill, have an accident, or suffer a terrible tragedy. They do guide us when it is appropriate for them to do so, but we must be open to their guidance by following our intuition and remaining aware of the signs, coincidences, and messengers they send plus the circumstances in which we find ourselves.

5. *"I was greeted by loved ones who passed before me when I returned home to the spirit world."* Our loved ones in spirit commonly want us to know that they were greeted by loved ones who passed before them upon their return to the afterlife. They often refer to this as a homecoming celebration, where family members, friends, and even pets greeted them with love and jubilance.

6. *"I am living in peace, joy, and love in the spirit world."* Although it is not possible to put into words the blissful experience of living in the

dimension of spirit, our deceased loved ones often try to convey to us how wonderful it is. They describe living in the light of the hereafter as feeling welcome, warm, safe, loved, joyful, boundless, liberated, peaceful, friendly, sweet, blissful, radiant, dreamlike, free, and harmonious, to list just a few of the common descriptions.

7. *"I love you."* As simple and basic as this may seem, love is the most important of all messages. Our loved ones in spirit always want us to know that they love us, which also means that they forgive us, they are proud of us, and they want nothing more for us than to be happy.

—☓—

Why don't psychic mediums accept the skeptics' challenges that offer monetary rewards for proving what they claim to do?

What I've learned in my investigation of the afterlife is that spirituality is a subjective experience, which means nobody is going to "prove" there is life after death. While there is plenty of evidence that we survive consciousness and that a spiritual dimension beyond our physical dimension exists, no one will ever be able to prove it to the masses because proof is a subjective term, while evidence is objective.

In this way, one person could witness a reading of spirit communication with a medium and say that the evidential messages equal proof of an afterlife (for him), while another person can conclude that the same messages do not equal proof (for her).

Therefore, no medium is ever going to be able to prove to a skeptic that they truly communicate with spirits because any skeptic who offers such a challenge has already made up their mind (what I refer to as a closed-minded skeptic), which is why they are willing to offer the monetary reward in the first place. They know proof is subjective, so they know they'll never have to pay the reward.

Sadly, these challenges are less about the skeptic actually seeking proof and more about them seeking publicity. It's just good sensational news, so it works in their favor.

—⧖—

What are psychic medium demonstrations?

A demonstration of mediumship (or medium demonstration) is an event where a psychic medium stands in front of a group of people, usually onstage, to randomly perform short (3- to 10-minute) readings for a few of the audience members. Medium demonstrations are similar to radio shows where mediums take callers, but this is a live public event where people can witness the spirit communication in person.

Three of the best mediums I've personally seen demonstrate onstage are John Holland (author of *Born Knowing*), James Van Praagh (author of *Talking to Heaven*), and John Edward (author of *One Last Time*). I think they are equally gifted, although their personalities are quite different and one might resonate with you more than the others. If you get a chance to see any of these mediums live, I encourage you to go.

—⧖—

What's the purpose of psychic medium demonstrations?

The purpose of a public demonstration of mediumship is *not* to give everyone in the audience a reading. That is what many attendees hope for when attending a medium demonstration, but this is not a forum for discounted private readings. The purpose of a public medium demonstration is to open people's minds to the possibilities—the possibility that an afterlife exists and spirit communication is achievable.

Personally, I believe that medium demonstrations are a stepping-stone toward the private reading, sort of like a sample that allows you to see if you want to make the full investment in the real thing. If you are skeptical, demonstrations allow you to witness other people getting readings. You might even get a short reading yourself. With any luck, the medium demonstration will provide you with the evidence required for you to think to yourself, *This might actually be real. I think I'll give a one-hour private reading a try.*

Medium demonstrations can also help people overcome their fear of spirit communication. By watching other people receive messages from the other side, fearful audience members might recognize that their fears are based on a lack of knowledge—fear of the unknown. Once these fears have been overcome, some people will be ready for a private reading with a medium.

For some, medium demonstrations are simply a form of entertainment, something to do on a Friday night. Yet these people are the minority. The majority of attendees go to a medium demonstration with a purpose. Some desperately want to communicate with someone they have lost. Some are seeking evidence of an afterlife to know that their deceased loved ones live on. Still, others want evidence to know that they, personally, will live on when they reach the end of this lifetime. And finally, some seek insight regarding life after death that will help them move forward in their bereavement process.

Whatever your reason for attending a medium demonstration, I highly recommend it. It is one of the most rewarding, educational, and thought-provoking experiences you can have on a Friday or Saturday night. Even if you leave the medium demonstration with remaining skepticism, you will be one step closer to that understanding that I like to call a "knowing." First, we are "skeptics." Then we become "believers." And in the end, if we have witnessed enough evidence to overcome a lifetime of limiting beliefs and learned skepticism, we become "knowers"—we know that spirit communication is real and that we survive death.

PART EIGHT

—ɷ—

QUESTIONS ABOUT SUICIDE AND MURDER

What happens in the afterlife to people who take their own life (suicide)?

In the overall picture, people who take their own life go to the spirit world like anyone else. And whatever was tormenting them that led them to take their own life is no longer a threat or issue. They are met with instant calm and peace. They are welcomed by loved ones who passed before them. And they are steeped in the unconditional love of Source light.

Despite some religious beliefs claiming that suicides go to hell, I've never uncovered any evidence that people who take their own life go to any place that could be described as hell. In fact, I've found no evidence whatsoever that hell exists at all for anyone, regardless of their choices or actions here on earth.

Having said that, there are aftereffects from the action of taking one's own life. Once a person who dies by suicide arrives in the afterlife, they will know instantly that their suicide was an act of free will, not a natural death. And because they, as spirits, are still connected to their human life, they might have regrets, but not in the way that you and I have regrets here on the physical plane.

Since souls have a human life in order to have experiences, their suicide is still an experience that teaches them something—they will learn and evolve from the experience. And some of what they learn is what the consequences are for themselves and others for making this choice to take their own life.

Having said all this, the fact is that this answer cannot be properly explained without reiterating the differences between the spirit and the soul because the spirit and the soul have different responses to suicide. You can reread more about the roles of the spirit and the soul in the "Big-Picture Answers" section at the beginning of this book. But I will reiterate some of what's written there to fully explain this important answer.

The soul is the equivalent of the higher self. The soul is always in the spirit world. And it is that part of us that has experienced many lifetimes. When it is ready to experience a new life, a part of the soul becomes the spirit that will enter the human body for that lifetime. As described earlier in this book, in this way, the spirit is the wave, and the soul is the ocean. The spirit (wave) is that part of the soul (ocean) that travels to the physical world (shore) to experience it.

The spirit extends beyond its whole self (the soul) to experience a human life—a *single* human life. Once that life is over, the spirit does not reincarnate to experience other lifetimes. Instead, the soul creates a new spirit of itself for each individual lifetime that it experiences.

Therefore, technically, our soul reincarnates, but our spirit does not. Yet because the spirit and the soul are one, the spirit feels as if it too is experiencing another life, just as each wave knows what the other waves are experiencing due to their oneness and connection with the ocean. And this is why there is so much confusion around the difference between spirit and soul—because they are distinct, but they are the same.

Thus, when a person's body dies, its spirit leaves the physical body to travel back into the spirit world and rejoin its soul. Yet the spirit's remerging with the soul does not eliminate the spirit; rather, the spirit always remains in the spirit world as one personality (among many) of its soul.

A helpful comparison, although not a perfect one, is when we grow old enough to leave our family. Think of the family unit as the soul and each individual member of the family as a spirit. We leave the family unit (soul) to go out and experience life on our own (spirit). But when we return to our family unit, we still retain our individuality. We are part of the family, yet we also have our own individualness.

So I am an Olson, but I am also Bob. The Olsons (comparing this to my soul) are experiencing many lives: one as me, one as my father, one as my mother, one as my sister, and so on. But I (comparing this to my spirit) am always Bob. Even when Bob returns home to the Olsons, Bob does not disappear. The same is true when your spirit returns to your soul. Your spirit is part of something greater than itself (your soul), but its individuality always remains.

Let's now discuss how the soul responds to its spirit taking its own life.

The soul has an acceptance for all physical experiences. Therefore, to the soul, the act of suicide is one of many experiences in a human's lifetime. The soul doesn't judge it, regret it, or approve of it. The soul can only accept it from a place of love. It becomes one more experience from which the soul will learn and grow because the soul learns from both sad and tragic experiences as much as happy and triumphant experiences.

The spirit, on the other hand, characterizes a more human perspective to its physical lifetime, so the spirit views the act of taking its life with a level of self-reproach. While the spirit retains a spiritual objectivity now that it has left the physical body, it also preserves a firm memory of its recent human life in order to gain the most advantageous benefits from its human experiences. In this way, the spirit will identify with a level of sorrow and remorse around its final human act.

The primary source of the spirit's self-reproach derives from its life review, which is that process every spirit experiences after leaving its physical body and returning home to the spiritual world. In the life review, the spirit learns how its choices and actions as a human being affected other people and the world.

Therefore, once the person who has taken his life goes through his life review, he now knows the anguish and grief he has caused his loved ones on the earth plane due to the suicide. And this is likely the worst of his load to carry as their suffering has only begun. Even though he now exists in the spiritual dimension where there is no time, he knows that his loved ones in the physical dimension do experience time. And it will take a lot of time for them to recover from his suicide if they ever do in their lifetime.

So spirits carry this weight of their suicide immediately following their passing, but only for a purpose. Since the act of suicide has many consequences, the spirit wants to know the experience from every angle. This is how they most evolve from the experience. If there were nothing to gain, the spirit would have the same objective acceptance of suicide as the soul. But the spirit-world experience is a continuation of the physical experience. It's like the aftershow that follows the main event (the human lifetime).

There are many people who believe that spirits who took their life as humans exist in hospital-like settings and require special care due to their low, almost-comatose energy and self-loathing atonement. That is not what my investigation into the afterlife has suggested. Quite the contrary, my investigation of the afterlife leads me to believe that everyone who crosses over to the spirit world—in spite of the cause or circumstances of their death—enters the spirit world surrounded by love, joy, and peace. But let me explain this more deeply.

As spirits, we are multidimensional beings. So while there is an aspect of our reentry into the afterlife that deals with our suicide as I just described, there are also other aspects to our spirit that have nothing to do with the suicide.

This means that our suicide experience is only one aspect of our entire lifetime. In other words, everything that we accomplished in our human life that just ended—all the love we gave to people, all the good deeds we spread among humanity, and all the joy we brought to our family members and friends—is not lost simply because our last act was to take our own life. While the suicide is significant and it certainly ends our spirit's human experience, it does not erase all our good choices and actions that took place before we died.

In fact, for our spirit, it is exactly all these positive and wonderful memories of our life that ease any anguish of our final act that might exist. All the lessons that we learned, the mistakes that taught us wisdom, the pain that made us compassionate, and the epiphanies that awakened us each remind us that the life we lived is meaningful regardless of how it ended.

As I alluded to earlier, what's important to realize is that no one dies by suicide if suicide is not a potential for that spirit's experience. There are some people who simply would never consider taking their own life. It's not in their nature. It's not in their genetic makeup. It's not a potential for their human experience. So for those who are wired in such a way that suicide is a temptation, it is only because suicide was something their soul chose as a potential for their life.

So if we came into this life with the potential of taking our own life, that also means that our friends and relatives came into this life with the potential that they might experience losing a loved one due to suicide. These people knew before they were born that this might be a potential experience for them as human beings. And they chose this as a possibility because it was an experience that would benefit them as eternal spiritual beings; that is, it was an experience they were willing to know because it would teach them about compassion, love, and respect for the human experience by knowing loss, grief, helplessness, and hopefully (at some point), surrender, acceptance, and forgiveness.

I actually have personal experience regarding the subject of suicide. Two decades ago, I suffered with clinical depression. My suffering was severe enough that the depression debilitated me for five years because my doctors could not find a successful treatment. I eventually found a treatment that lifted my depression and has left me depression-free since 1994. But I was challenged during those five years with the temptation to take my life in order to escape my suffering.

During that time of my life, I dealt with what is called suicidal ideation—persistent thoughts of taking my own life. I therefore came into this world with the potential of taking my life. Likewise, my wife, Melissa, came into this life with the potential of grieving my loss in the way that only suicide survivors can know. The same is true for all my family members and friends.

In my case, I met the challenge by not taking my life, though I admit it could have gone either way at times. I'm grateful for the sake of both Melissa and myself that I overcame that challenge. But I know it was an experience that both our souls were prepared to endure. That's what human life is all about. I have no doubt that my soul will be better off that I did not succumb to the temptation of suicide. At least I know my spirit won't have to deal with the suicide-related self-reproach I noted earlier.

I have now discussed the best and the worst of what a spirit will experience in response to their suicide. Keep in mind that a spirit's reasons for self-reproach are not a requirement and only exist for the spirit to extract the greatest benefits from this previous human lifetime, which include everything that a spirit can learn from the act of suicide. And when the spirit grows from an experience, so does the soul.

The spirit's reaction to its suicide is not a whole lot different from the way we feel about our choices here on the earth plane. It's common to hear someone say something like "Well, there's one part of me that feels really guilty about stealing that car when I was 17, but there's another part of me that has learned from that experience and grown from it. So I'm also glad that I did it in spite of the fact that I went to jail for two months and brought shame upon my family. I'm now a better person overall for having had that difficult experience."

In the spirit world, we are so multidimensional that there are countless parts of us that deal with every aspect of our choices, suicide included. So on one level, we'll feel deep regret for taking our life. On another level, we'll feel sadness and compassion for our surviving loved ones. On another level, we'll feel gratitude for the life we lived. On another level, we'll feel peace for being back home in the afterlife. On another level, we'll feel pleased for our positive accomplishments in that life. And on still another level, we'll feel displeasure for our other poor choices that hurt others in that lifetime. We are multidimensional spiritual beings, so we experience our entire lifetime from many different perspectives.

What I'll say in conclusion here is that over the course of our many human lives, the probability is that each one of us has been a murderer, a rapist, and a thief as well as a humanitarian, a guardian, and a philanthropist. And it's quite possible, if not probable, that you took your own life during one of your many lifetimes. That means your soul, your higher self, was all of those things in other lifetimes, yet you are still who you are today—even in this lifetime—because of what you as a soul learned and how you grew as a result of those experiences.

So if you are worried that your loved one who took their life is suffering some torturous eternal hell, from a practical standpoint alone, it might help to consider that his soul has likely endured worse in other lifetimes. Pray for him, of course, but find peace in knowing these key points that I will repeat here:

1. Your loved one's suicide is only one aspect of his life. There were many other aspects that made his life meaningful and beneficial to his soul, none of which are discounted by his final act.

2. Your loved one's suicide was always a potential that was predetermined by his soul before his birth. It was a challenge for him to meet, and even though his free will chose the path he did, it is still a path

that will provide his soul with lessons, wisdom, and compassion that he'll carry with him for all eternity.

3. Your loved one's soul has endured many lives and expressed its free will in many unflattering, reprehensible, and even shameful ways—just like the rest of us—but that is part of experiencing a human life. His choice to take his life during this lifetime is only one aspect of his multidimensional being, which means that he will also know the peace, love, and joy of the afterlife like everyone else, just like his soul has done many times after innumerable human lifetimes.

—〰—

What happens in the afterlife if someone commits suicide due to a mental illness or addiction?

People who complete suicide due to a mental illness still go through the same processes as anyone who takes their own life, but they are influenced by the illness, which means there will be less reason for self-reproach.

This is one of those situations where the person was challenged with the potential for suicide. Every spirit hopes to get through their mental illness without taking their life, but it certainly is taken into account when they are going through their life review and judging themself regarding their choices (take note: judging themself, not being judged by others).

I say this as someone who has suffered with clinical depression, so I understand that there are times when suicidal ideation is more conscious than other times. What I mean here is that the influence of mental illness fluctuates, so there are times when it has more of a subconscious influence and times when it has much less of a hold. Considering this, one can't use their mental illness as an excuse to take their life without any effect in the afterlife. A lot depends on the degree of control that the mental illness has on one's conscious choices. And we don't get away with anything once in the spirit world—our spirit and soul, as well as our spirit guides, always see the truth with the utmost clarity.

People under the influence of mental illness—indisputably, depression—are typically fixated on escaping their pain. Their thoughts are characteristically irrational, which can cause them to hyperfocus on their problems and suffering. The idea of how their suicide will affect their loved ones is likely to never enter their mind at the time of the act. At the very least, their decision making is critically clouded by their state of mind. I know that this was my experience during my five-year depression, and my research has indicated that this is typical.

I mention this because I know a lot of people ask, "How could she do this to me?" But the reality is that she likely didn't have the clarity of mind to be thinking of other people. Instead, she was more likely laser-focused on escaping the torment of her depression. Consequently (and again, I'm speaking from personal experience), I encourage you to not take their suicide as a measure of how much they loved or cared about you. Mental illness has a way of provoking people so deeply that they are unable to fully consider how their act of suicide will affect others. It's sad—I know. And it is unfair on so many levels. But it's the reality of mental illness.

—∿∿—

What happens in the afterlife if someone purposely took drugs but accidentally overdosed or purposely drove while drunk but accidentally got into a fatal accident?

In the case of accidental deaths that were precipitated by a conscious act that is known to potentially lead to such accidents, the person in spirit always accepts some responsibility. While this is not the same as consciously taking their own life, people in spirit usually accept responsibility for their death in these cases and, as a result, feel the weight of what they did, which includes feeling responsible for their loved ones' grief.

I answer this question, however, having explained the multidimensional aspects of our soul in the question about suicide. The same principles apply here. Our existence in the spirit world is not all gloom and regret for our choices and actions here as humans. There is always an aspect of love, joy, peace, and safety for every person in spirit. But feeling how their actions affected others on the physical plane is a big part of the life review experience. And in cases like this, it can be a difficult experience to know.

—∾—

What happens to criminals and murderers in the afterlife?

I recommend that you read my answer above about suicide before reading this one as the answer I gave for people who take their own life is also true for people who take the lives of others, including mass murderers. But I like this question because the answer provides a deeper understanding of the spirit's and soul's perspectives.

While it is absolutely true that taking another person's life is never acceptable from a human perspective—and there will always be consequences felt by the spirit of the person who takes a life—these consequences have everything to do with the murderer's spirit judging and punishing himself and nothing to do with him being judged or punished by some higher spiritual being.

As mentioned elsewhere in this book, the reason there is no punishment in the spirit world (as most people believe or expect) is because there is no hell. The only hell that exists is the one we create for ourselves, which can be quite harsh in itself. Nevertheless, criminals and murderers go to the afterlife like everyone else, yet they will surely face the truth about the suffering they caused others through their crimes. To their spirits, this can be challenging, even harrowing. But to their souls, it is purely another experience from which to learn and grow, even though all souls have immense love and compassion for human beings.

Understanding Potentials …

Because humans have free will, spirits enter a physical body, and therefore a human life, only with the *potential* to be a murderer. I use the word 'potential' because our human free will makes most pre-birth plans a probability rather than a certainty.

As I described in my answer regarding suicide, what's important to keep in mind is that no one commits murder if being a murderer is not a potential for that spirit's experience. There are some people who simply would never consider taking another person's life. It's not in their nature or genetic makeup. It's simply not a potential for their human experience. So for those who are created in such a way that they *might* kill another person (due to an uncontrollable temper, lack of respect for human life, or deep-rooted greed or hatred), it is only because killing another person was something their soul chose as a potential for their life.

When we, as souls, choose to have a human life, we come here with a plan. Within that plan, there are potential experiences that we *might* come to know. We might know love, or we might know hatred. We might know health, or we might know sickness. We might know companionship, or we might know loneliness. We might know respect for human life, or we might know disdain for human life.

Our potentials are part of our energetic makeup, but we, as souls, also set up the particulars of our lifetime in order to shape our potentials, yet without influencing them one way or the other. For instance, our souls choose for us certain parents, siblings, genetics, socioeconomic backgrounds, and physical appearances, to name just a few examples out of the unlimited that exist. All these choices are purposeful in order to provide us with the physical experiences that we, as souls, wish to have and know, experiences that we simply cannot have as nonphysical beings who exist in the ever-loving, joyful, peaceful, and safe environment of the afterlife.

The only variable that exists when we, as souls, plan our human life is that we never know exactly how we might act in reference to any one potential. This is because we have free will as human beings. And it is our free will that makes human life so intriguing to our souls because it ultimately determines what side of every potential we'll choose. Free will is the one freedom humans have that makes life so unpredictable. Otherwise, everything would be determined by fate.

So if a person came into this life with the potential of taking another person's life, that also means that the murderer's victim came into this life with the potential of ending his life in this way. This is not to say that he wanted to be murdered. Certainly, his human self didn't want it. And this doesn't necessarily mean that both souls had a pre-birth agreement that one would kill the other, although that can happen. But one person's potential met the other person's potential like energetic puzzle pieces that attracted one another, created a match, and fit together to result in an outcome that both souls accepted as a potential in their human lives.

In this same manner, if a person murders someone, that murderer's friends and relatives came into this life with the potential that they might experience having a friend or relative who becomes a murderer. The souls (and spirits) of these people knew before they were born that this *might* be a potential experience for them as human beings. And they chose this as a possibility because it was an experience that would progress their evolution as eternal spiritual beings; that is, it was an experience they were willing to know because it would teach them about compassion, love, and respect for the human experience by knowing loss, grief, fear, helplessness, and hopefully (at some point, depending upon the situation), surrender, acceptance, and forgiveness.

From a Spirit Perspective ...

When one human carries out a potential by actually taking another person's life, that person's spirit is not immune to the consequences of this act just because the spirit now exists on the spiritual plane.

The spirit characterizes a more human perspective to its physical lifetime than the soul, so the spirit views the act of taking someone's life with a level of self-reproach. While the spirit retains a spiritual objectivity now that it has left the physical body, it also preserves a firm memory of its recent human life in order to gain the most evolution from its human experiences. In this way, the spirit will identify with a level of sorrow and remorse around its human act of murder, even if that spirit didn't feel these emotions as a human. And the spirit will know these feelings because of the wide and insightful perspective it gains during its life review.

As you now know if you've read this book from the beginning, the spirit undergoes an emotional life review by feeling the consequences of its actions (the murder) as well as feeling the ripple effect from all the other humans affected. This includes the range of emotions felt by people who grieved the victim's passing, people who witnessed the murder, people who became fearful just by learning about the murder, people who were inspired to copy the crime as well as that copycat's murder victims, and others. Few of us know how many people we affect with our actions, positively or negatively, but we find out during the life review.

Once the person who has taken a life goes through his life review, he now knows the anguish and grief he has caused people still living on the earth plane due to his actions. And this might be the worst of his burden. Although he now exists in the spiritual dimension where there is no time, he knows that people in the physical dimension do experience time. And many loved ones of murder victims never fully recover. At the very least, the experience causes each one of them a level of suffering that this murderer's spirit will now know.

It's important that I emphasize that the spirit's afterlife experience (including the life review) is an *extension* of its human life experience. This means that knowing how its human choices and actions affected others is a valuable piece to that lifetime experience. Said another way, the afterlife experience of the spirit is as important as the physical life experience. It's a continuation of it.

Therefore, whatever suffering a spirit endures by knowing how its act of murder affected others is not so much a punishment than it is a furtherance of the learning and evolvement from that lifetime. While it might be a difficult process to endure, it is how our spirit fully benefits from its human lifetime. And this is as true for murder as it is for suicide or any human action that we might consider wrong, immoral, or bad.

Finally, just as I mentioned in my answer about suicide, no human life is evaluated by the spirit based on one act alone. Many murders result from an outburst of anger or are influenced by alcohol, drugs, or one of many mental health issues. In other words, many of these people have a lifetime of other behavior that might include acts of kindness, generosity, and love. And these positive choices and actions are also part of their life review. So the spirits of these people will feel the ripple effects of this conduct as well, which adds to the growth gained from the lifetime as a whole.

From a Soul Perspective ...

The soul's perspective of a human life is more objective. While the soul does not approve of murder, the soul accepts it. In this way, the soul takes this human tragedy and extracts any learning and evolution it can from the experience.

Murder and all human experiences that result from this act (for example, people's grief, the murderer's prison sentence, the fear felt by people who witnessed the crime) are experiences that are foreign to spiritual beings in their dimension—because there is no murder or crime in the afterlife. Therefore, from this experience, the soul learns about hate, love, fear, bravery, grief, loss, forgiveness, vengeance, compassion, and so much more.

So viewing this subject from the soul's perspective (because any human lifetime is only a brief moment in a soul's eternal existence), the soul does not view the murder the same way we do. The soul gets to live a physical life again and again, so it views all human acts from a more impartial perspective, much more so than the spirit.

Still, to keep this in perspective and not paint the picture that our souls are uncaring, heartless beings, our souls know nothing but love. They are the embodiment of compassion. And because we are connected to our souls so much more intimately than we can ever recognize, our souls have immense empathy for our suffering.

So from a human perspective, what any murderer does is evil and intolerable. And as a human being, I fully agree with this conviction. But our souls are not without compassion either. Souls completely understand the pain and suffering humans experience as a result of these horrific crimes. So I can assure you that no one in either dimension is making light of anyone's suffering due to a homicide or any crime.

What This Can Teach Us …

Whenever we contemplate the afterlife in reference to the big questions like murder and suicide, if we can find it within ourselves to step back from our human emotional responses for just a moment, we will be able to glimpse the wisdom that this insight provides, which is that these horrendous events teach both spirit and soul as much about the human perspective of good as they do the human perspective of evil. In fact, the reason our souls choose to have these experiences is because it's necessary to experience all sides of it in order to fully know it. This is why Source allows suffering, war, and hate in the world just as it allows joy, peace, and love. As I wrote at the beginning of this book, life is about experiences. It's not just about having happy experiences; it's about having—and knowing—all experiences.

What I'll say in conclusion here is exactly what I said in the question on suicide, which is that over the course of our many human lives, the probability is that each one of us has been a murderer, a rapist, and a thief as well as a humanitarian, a guardian, and a philanthropist. This means that your soul has likely known all these experiences in other lifetimes, yet you are still who you are today because of what you as a soul learned and how you grew as a result of those experiences.

So whatever our human feelings are around criminals or murderers, and as justified as those feelings may be, understanding that each of us has likely been a criminal and murderer in other lifetimes might possibly help us to balance our anger and animosity with emotions that are healthier and more constructive. That's the takeaway from learning about the afterlife. No one is suggesting that it's easy or even necessary, but it's a goal for which to strive, especially if you recognize that concepts like forgiveness and acceptance are as much for your benefit as they are for all humanity.

—☶—

Do criminals and murderers meet up with their victims in the afterlife?

Yes. In fact, the murderer and the murder victim might have met before they were ever born. As souls, one might have agreed to be the murderer, and the other agreed to be the murder victim. In some situations, they'll plan to be family members, friends, or lovers. In other cases, they'll plan to be strangers or distant acquaintances.

But this is not always the case. Sometimes a soul will go into a life with the "potential" to be murdered or the "potential" to be a murderer. In these cases, what happens is left up to the choices of those people. Depending upon their freewill choices and depending upon how their spirit guides guide them to be in certain places at certain times, someone might be murdered in a way that appears quite happenstance when it's really no accident from a spirit-world perspective.

In these cases, one spirit came into this world with the potential to be a murderer, and another person came into this world with the potential to be murdered. Taking this a step further, every friend and relative in these two people's lives came into the world either with the potential to know the murderer or know the murder victim. Why would they do that? Because being a family member or friend of a murderer is one experience, while being a family member or friend of a person who is murdered is a completely different experience. And since the purpose of life is experience, those people's souls are possibly experiencing those things for the first time (or in a different way than ever before).

So regardless of whether they preplanned this together or simply planned for the *potential* in their life, it's possible, although not necessary, that they later met in the spirit world after their lives. But that meeting wouldn't play out the way most people would expect it to unfold, meaning the murderer wouldn't likely be apologizing while the murder victim was chastising. Instead, they might actually meet as two souls who played a significant role in one another's life. They might even compare notes about their experiences in order to learn from the experience from both sides and at a deeper level.

In some cases, the two souls (murder victim and murderer) might have shared many lifetimes together. There's evidence from spirit communication with mediums, near-death experiences, and life-between-lives regressions that many of us tend to hang out in soul groups in which we share multiple lifetimes together (while switching roles from lifetime to lifetime). So in one life, Soul A might be the father, and Soul B might be the son. And in another life, Soul A and Soul B might be friends, coworkers, lovers, in-laws, or enemies. They'll even switch gender, race, and class. Or they might be strangers until their paths meet one day and something significant like the murder occurs.

—⟋⟋⟍—

What happens in the afterlife when someone kills another due to a mental illness or addiction?

As mentioned in the similar question on suicide, a lot depends upon the level at which the mental illness or addiction influenced the free-will choice of that person doing the killing. As a spirit reviewing the incident, this influence will affect the accountability.

This, of course, does not change the fact that one human killed another human. That person's spirit will feel the human consequences of his actions. There is no get-out-of-jail-free card just because someone was influenced by the mental illness or addiction. The spirit, and those spiritual beings working with him, will know the truth with crystal clarity as to how much influence was involved.

Free will is also involved when a person has the opportunity to treat their mental illness or addiction and chooses against it—or chooses to drink before driving or take the drugs. Sometimes this choice is a fully conscious one; sometimes it too is influenced by the illness or addiction. But it's not really our concern here since the truth cannot be hidden once in spirit. Even if we as humans are unable to determine true accountability, we'll see right to the core of the issue when in spirit.

—∞—

What happens in the afterlife if someone took another's life by accident?

When deaths occur without intention or reckless abandonment, it is tragedy without blame. These experiences serve to teach all the people involved lessons that they came into this lifetime to know. If you understood the idea of potential as I described it in the last few answers, you'll see how it applies here too. The souls of those involved preplanned the event—or something like it—in order to know an experience from a different angle, learn a lesson, balance karma, or heal something.

When a child darts in front of a car and is killed, for example, the driver of that car undergoes a difficult experience that can challenge that person for life. Part of the challenge for the driver during his life will be to forgive himself for the accident. He'll need to overcome the questions that repeat in his head: Could I have been paying better attention? Would this have happened if I had replaced my brake pads when the mechanic suggested it? Was I driving too fast? Did that single glass of wine affect my reaction time?

The driver may have to face the child's grieving family too. He'll have to move on with his life and learn to feel happiness again in spite of the parents' possible inability to move forward and be happy again. He might even feel the brunt of the parents' hostility toward him. Or the parents could take compassion for his distress and forgive him for the death of their child. This would be a completely different experience.

In cases like these, the experience is a human one only, meaning the driver will only struggle with that event while in physical form.

But once in spiritual form, his torment of responsibility will end because the driver's spirit will understand that it was not his fault. That spirit will see with clarity that the child's soul preplanned its early departure, just as the driver's soul preplanned this experience of taking another's life accidentally. The two souls' pre-birth plans (potentials) met to create the human tragedy.

If the driver did drink alcohol or was driving over the speed limit, there might be some accountability for those freewill choices at a spirit level. But if the accident was fulfilling the pre-birth plans of both souls, that negligence will likely have no effect on a spiritual level. Instead, those choices might be mere coincidence or might have allowed the preplanned outcome to occur. So while the possibilities are infinite, you probably now understand the bigger picture of how this works.

—⁂—

What happens to soldiers who kill others in war?

Again, it's important to read the previous answers in this section as they will paint the bigger picture. If you have read these, you already know that there is no eternal damnation for soldiers who killed during wartime. But there are many aspects of this question that cannot be described here as I could possibly write an entire book on it due to the many possibilities that exist for soldiers during war.

For example, some soldiers kill because they were ordered to kill, others kill out of fear of being killed, and still others kill innocent people (women and children, for instance) because they are overwhelmed and stressed and are thinking irrationally from the pressures and difficulties of war. Each reason for killing will hold a different energy and have a different sense of accountability and, therefore, will be a different experience for that spirit.

Generally, however, killing in war holds greater similarity to killing by accident than, say, murder. It is an experience that their souls chose to know. Typically, it isn't a killing based on evil intentions. It's more likely acted upon out of patriotism, protection of country, loyalty to leaders, and fear of being killed. These are quite different intentions for killing than vengeance, hatred, greed, or criminality.

Souls in this situation choose to know the experience of being a soldier in wartime. They know that having a human life at this time in history—and with all the other preplanned selections within which they are born—means they are likely to become soldiers and go to war. And they choose it because it provokes human freewill choices that we can't know in normal life outside of war.

Facing death the way soldiers do is a unique experience. Friends and comrades are dying beside them. They are forced to choose survival at times or risk their life to save another's. They must kill other human beings for the mere fact that their military leaders told them to do so or because those humans might kill them, all the while knowing that the enemy soldier likely has parents, siblings, spouses, and children who love and will grieve that person's death.

Killing in war is a human experience like no other. And just as I wrote about the driver who accidentally killed a child, this is more of a human experience than a spiritual one, meaning the experience ends when the soldier who killed another dies. While that soldier's spirit will come to know how the people he killed felt when he killed them and how that person's loved ones felt upon learning of his death, it will typically be an easy transition to self-forgiveness and self-compassion. This spirit will know that his soul purposely planned this war experience, and he will fully recognize how limited any soldier feels in his choices.

To the person's soul (not spirit), however, the entire ordeal is an accepted experience—it isn't good, bad, or indifferent. Just the fact that the soul signed up to have this experience—one of the most difficult challenges a human can know—says a lot about that soul's sense of courage, strength, adventure, and dedication to growth.

PART NINE

—⚬—

QUESTIONS ABOUT PAST LIVES AND REINCARNATION

What are past lives?

Past lives are lifetimes that our soul has experienced during a physical-world era that dates before our current lifetime. As discussed in the beginning of this book (in the section "Big-Picture Answers"), Source creates souls, and souls create spirits, and it is spirits that inhabit physical bodies when experiencing human lifetimes. In fact, as explained in the "Big-Picture Answers" section, the soul creates a new spirit to experience every new lifetime.

According to people who have had near-death experiences (NDEs), the term 'past lives' is a bit of an inaccuracy from a spiritual perspective. Because NDEs teach us that there is no time (or distance) in the spiritual realm, this means there is no past or future in the spirit world—everything is happening at the same time. Consequently, there really are no past lives, only "other" lives.

On the other hand, because we are humans and we must live with linear time, the concept of past lives is completely accurate from our viewpoint, which is why I'm going to continue discussing "*other* lives" using the phrase '*past* lives.' Just keep in mind that this is "true but not accurate" from a spiritual-realm perspective. The phrase 'other lives' is more accurate than 'past lives.'

—⟋⟍—

What's the connection between past lives and reincarnation?

Early in my investigation of life after death, I interviewed a lot of people about their beliefs regarding the afterlife. One of my early questions during these interviews was if the interviewees believed in past lives. Almost every person I interviewed said yes. Later in the interviews, I asked them if they believed in reincarnation. Astonishingly, most of these same people said no.

I always found that amusing since past lives and reincarnation go hand in hand. If you believe that we have lived past lives, then by default, you believe in reincarnation. Most dictionaries define reincarnation as "rebirth of a soul in a new body," which is a pretty good definition. I would only emphasize that the soul enters the physical body through a spirit.

The reason most of these people said they don't believe in reincarnation, I presume, is because their religion told them that believing in reincarnation is wrong. Nonetheless, this is obviously one of those instances where people's core beliefs are in conflict with what they've been told by their religious teachers—they believe in past lives but don't believe in reincarnation.

In a nutshell, reincarnation simply means that our souls experience more than one lifetime, which equates to us having past lives.

—⟋⟍—

What evidence is there for reincarnation and past lives?

The most compelling evidence we have for reincarnation and past lives is from past-life regressions and past-life memories.

PAST-LIFE REGRESSION: The first evidence we have for past lives (and, therefore, reincarnation) is past-life regression. I put this evidence first because anyone can experience a past-life regression. A past-life regression is when a person is guided into a meditative state of mind with verbal imagery and then experiences a past life through hypnotic suggestion.

Hypnotic suggestion, however, only suggests the direction to take your focus without offering any details of what that experience will be like. For example, the hypnotic regressionist might suggest that a person "remember their most recent past life." The key is that the regressionist is not making any suggestions of what that most recent past life looks like, sounds like, smells like, tastes like, or feels like. The hypnotic suggestion is merely the vehicle that steers them to that past-life memory by suggesting the person go there.

I have experienced past-life regressions myself. These are some of the most eye-opening, life-changing experiences of my life. In my first regression, I could feel what it felt like to be in the body of a guy named George from a Celtic land in 1643. I had an inner knowing of what his personality was like—joyful, friendly, and happy-go-lucky. And when English soldiers ambushed George's townspeople during a parade (killing many of his friends), I relived the frenzy in my mind. I could feel the grief and horror that George felt during that experience and after it. And I literally had a visceral experience in the regression-ist's office where I cried, shivered, and shook.

While this description doesn't paint an attractive picture, this was a fascinating experience that taught me a lot. Even more than that, this experience gave me evidence of past lives and reincarnation. It was a personal experience that provided me with a knowing about past lives, meaning I know that past lives exist. Of course, it was *my* experience and, therefore, *my* evidence, meaning it would not serve as evidence for anyone else. In order for past-life regression to be evidence for other people, each person needs to experience it for himself or herself. Nevertheless, it is persuasive evidence that past lives exist.

PAST-LIFE MEMORY: The second evidence for past lives is past-life memory. Past-life memory is when a person recalls memories of a past life, meaning that they remember details about the past life as if they were remembering what happened to them yesterday.

This is more common with children than adults because we tend to forget our past-life memories as we get older. The theory is that children recall their past lives more often than adults because they have only been away from the spirit world a short time—the veil between the spiritual realm and the physical realm is thinner. It seems that the older we get, the more we forget.

One of the earliest documented cases of past-life memory occurred with a woman named Jenny Cockell. Although she grew up and lives in England, Jenny recalled her life as Mary Sutton, an Irishwoman who died 21 years before Jenny was born. Because Mary left eight young children behind when she passed, her emotional concern about the children transferred to Jenny. As an adult, using maps she drew as a child from her past-life memories, Jenny Cockell traced her memories to the exact location where she lived in her past life, which is Malahide, Ireland. Thereafter, due to her diligent research, Jenny also located Mary's children and personally reunited with five of them (who, of course, were all older than her). You can read about Jenny's story in her best-selling book, *Across Time and Death: A Mother's Search for Her Past-Life Children*.

As mentioned at the beginning of this book, a more recent best-selling book titled *Soul Survivor*, by Bruce and Andrea Leininger, documents a boy's memory as a World War II pilot. The story is significant because the boy's parents eventually researched their son's claims (despite their skepticism). What they learned is that the man their son claimed to have been actually existed 60 years prior, and many details given by their son were eerily accurate.

Cases like these offer compelling evidence of past lives. Although someone might argue that there could be other reasons why these children know this information that was verified to be true (for example, a spirit might have impressed these memories upon the susceptible children's minds), the people who remember these memories typically feel they are past-life memories because of the emotion they feel in connection with them. Consequently, they instinctively feel that they were these people from this recent lifetime.

If you suspect that your child is having memories from a past life, Carol Bowman's book *Children's Past Lives: How Past Life Memories Affect Your Child* is an insightful resource.

—∿—

How many lives do we live?

If you understand the Source > Soul > Spirit hierarchy recapped throughout this book, then you might already recognize that our spirit will never live another life. Each spirit, which is sometimes referred to as a "personality," lives only one lifetime. But the soul of that spirit will likely live thousands or millions of lives—possibly infinite lives. Still, there is no conclusive answer to this question, and I'll explain why.

Our souls have the free will to stop living human lives if they choose. But that doesn't mean the soul won't continue to experience lives as other species. Many people who have had near-death experiences claim that we experience lifetimes as animals, insects, germs, plants, rocks, and even gases. They also tell us that we live lives of various sorts on other planets, in other universes, and even in other dimensions.

Many people ask, "How many lives do we live?" because their life has been extraordinarily challenging. These people are too tired and weary to imagine living another life. Their question is actually rooted in their hope that they won't reincarnate again because they can't fathom experiencing another difficult life.

These people should find comfort in knowing that your spirit will not live another lifetime—not technically. Your soul (your whole self) will, more likely than not, experience another human life via a new spirit, but the full personality that is you in this lifetime won't know that other lifetime the same way you know this one.

I'll use the ocean and wave analogy again because it works so well. You are a wave, but you are also one aspect of the ocean. The ocean is your whole self (soul). The water of the wave is not separate from the water of the ocean. Yet your experience as a wave feels quite separate. And when you, as a wave, roll up onto the shore and then back into the ocean, your life as that wave is over. But does the water of that wave disappear? Certainly not. It simply washes back into the ocean. The ocean will create more waves after you, but the entirety of the wave that was you (every molecule that formulated you) will never rush up on the shore again.

This, however, does not mean you won't be able to experience other lives. You certainly will. Because you are also your soul, you do experience other lives via a whole-self perspective. In fact, you'll get to experience any of your soul's lifetimes as closely or distantly as you choose because you are connected to that new spirit by sharing the same soul. So you, your soul, and all your soul's spirits are all connected as one. But your spirit has the option to remain as attached or unattached to any new lifetime exactly as you please.

So how many lifetimes might one soul experience? One near-death experiencer named Natalie Sudman, whom I've interviewed more than once, actually suggests that our souls might live out the infinite possibilities of every probable choice that is available to us. Described another way, we might live out the choice to go to college (the choice we did make) while also living out the choice to not go to college (the choice we didn't make in this lifetime). As Natalie described, she currently knows the Natalie who made the choices that are part of her awareness, but there might be additional Natalies who exist who made opposite choices—or other alternate choices.

It's a bit of a mind-boggling concept, I know, but it's an example of the possibilities. And it can be fun to contemplate these potentials because it breaks us out of the confines of our finite, structured beliefs. Yet even Natalie admitted—and I agree with her—that this concept of our soul living out every possible choice is fundamentally a meaningless notion to her in this life (or, should I say, in this awareness). It serves no purpose other than maybe the novelty of thinking that when we make an error of judgment, at least we probably made the correct choice in another version of our self.

Finally, in answering this question of how many lives we live, it's important to note that our soul can experience the lifetimes of other souls too while in the spirit world. Each soul shares the lifetimes of other souls like tapping into a virtual reality. And in the opposite way, we can also allow other souls to know our lifetimes. Simply by setting our intention to do so—and the other soul setting the intention to share a lifetime—we are able to download all the experiences and emotions of that lifetime. We can experience the lifetime in its entirety or only a small segment of it.

—〜〜—

How long do we wait while in spirit before entering another human life?

Since time doesn't exist in the spiritual realm, this question in itself is a misnomer. There is no past or future; there is only the present in the spirit world. Yet since our human brains really cannot fathom timelessness, I'll answer this as best I can from a human perspective.

Without getting too deep, let me just answer the question the way most people want it answered. From my own investigation of past lives, there doesn't seem to be any protocol on how long a soul must wait to experience another human life. So the possibilities are truly unlimited.

If you've been able to grasp what I've been teaching about the relationship between soul and spirit, then you probably understand now that our individual spirit does not reincarnate—only our soul does by creating a new spirit. Thus, in this way, there is no waiting period before entering another human life because the soul can experience multiple human lives at the same time—via multiple spirits.

I mentioned the wonderful book titled *Soul Survivor*, written by Bruce and Andrea Leininger, about the boy who recalled memories of his past life as a World War II pilot 60 years prior. Now that's a quick reincarnation. And in the other book I mentioned, *Across Time and Death* by Jenny Cockell, she recalled memories of her previous life, which was just 21 years after the death of Mary Sutton (the woman Jenny has vivid memories of being). She reincarnated so quickly that she reunited with her past-life children.

Many people ask this question because they're worried that their loved ones will reincarnate before they themselves physically die and return home to the spirit world. This, you might now realize, should not be a concern. Since it is our soul that reincarnates via another spirit—not our spirit itself—you are assured that your loved one will always be there to greet you when your life here is over as they (their spirit) remain in the spirit world for eternity.

—◊—

Do we really chart our lives in spirit before we're born?

Yes, with the help of our spiritual guides, elders, and masters, our souls plan our lives before we're born into them. Our souls know what we hope to accomplish in each lifetime, and so our souls set the stage for that to take place.

Our souls choose where on the planet we'll be born, including the culture, the socioeconomic background, the time in history, and any other major choices of this sort that will best shape the experiences our souls want us to have. With this information, our souls choose our parents and, therefore, our family, along with all the details, dysfunction, and deliciousness that comes with those choices. We are also born with the health or physical/mental conditions that will best lead us toward the physical experiences our souls wish to have during our lifetime.

Once we're born, we are guided by our spirit guides, who influence us to take the path that best supports the experiences we came here to experience. That doesn't mean we'll always follow that guidance (i.e., always listen to our intuition) because we have free will. But our guides do try to lead us in the right direction.

So if we don't like our parents, the location where we were born, or the body into which we were born, we have no one to blame but ourselves—that is, we can only blame our own souls.

—⟋⟍⟍—

Might my deceased child come back to me as my next child?

As I've been repeating in this book, anything is possible. I'm not sure it is likely, but I do think it's possible. But let's look at this question from different angles.

If the child did come back to you, it would be the soul of that child that would be returning. The spirit of the child (the true personality) itself would not return as spirits do not reincarnate. But whether it's the soul or the spirit, the spiritual core of that child is still the same.

Even though the spirit of the child would have its own personality, the soul has certain signature characteristics that are identifiable in every spirit connected to it. So there would be some characteristics that each spirit would share—similar to shared characteristics of a family. The point here is that if a soul were to reincarnate as a new child of bereaved parents, the child might be similar, but not the same as the first child.

What's important to keep in mind here is that your child that passed will remain in the spirit world even if its soul reincarnates back to you. This means you can talk to her in spirit or pray to her, and she will greet you when you return home upon your passing.

At the same time, if the soul really were to reincarnate in this way, since the child that passed shares the same soul with the newborn child, your child in spirit will experience all the love, joy, and challenges of the new child because of their soul connection. But this is true whether your new child is from the same soul as the passed child or not because the oneness of all souls and spirits holds a connection between all spiritual beings that cannot be described in human terms. Suffice it to say that all spirits, souls, and Source feel the love you give your child, regardless of their spiritual lineage to your child who passed.

I have two brothers in spirit who died at birth. One was born before me. The other was born after me. What's interesting is that my parents gave them the same name, Peter. The reason I mention it is because they often come through in my readings with mediums, and they come through as two personalities. The point being that even if they are both of the same soul (I don't know if they are or aren't), they present themselves as separate individuals. Thus, for the sake of example, if we assume that both Peters shared the same soul, my parents would not have been getting the Peter who died before me even if the second Peter had lived.

If you have lost a child, what I think is important to understand in this answer is that your child's passing has provided you with the experience of loss, which holds lessons that are beneficial to your eternal soul (as well as your child's soul). Your soul and your child's soul had a pre-birth agreement to give you the experience of loss and bereavement. It seems to me that having that exact same child return to you would be contradictory to that pre-birth plan.

While grieving the death of a child is unquestionably one of the most challenging experiences a soul can choose for a lifetime, it also infuses one's soul with immense compassion for others in the face of any loss. The experience teaches that soul about the value of time, the importance of present-moment awareness, the rewards of aging, and the power of love, to name just a few. I'm not sure if the spiritual growth that takes place after experiencing such a loss would hold the same lessons if the child returned as a future baby. My presumption is that the new child would be an entirely new experience that might even test the growth of the lessons learned from your loss. In this way, the new child gives you the opportunity to put those lessons into action.

—ɯ—

What is a past-life regression?

If you are still confused about what a past-life regression is at this point in this book, the following provides some extra information.

A past-life regression is a technique of hypnosis used to recall memories of previous lifetimes. It's completely safe, you are always in control (you can open your eyes and stop the regression at any time), and you are fully aware of what's going on around you during the regression. In fact, you have to be aware of what's going on because you are listening to the regressionist and answering any questions he is asking you.

The past-life regression begins with the hypnosis practitioner (hypnotist or hypnotherapist) reciting verbal imagery that leads you into a deep level of relaxation. Once you are deeply relaxed, the regressionist will often regress you to recall memories from this lifetime. You might recall memories from your childhood or even while in the womb. Once the regressionist feels you are ready, he will use more guided imagery to lead you into a past-life memory.

This sometimes begins by you visualizing a door opening, and on the other side of that door is a past life. Once the regressionist suggests that you walk through the door and into that past-life memory, he'll stop suggesting imagery and begin asking you questions about what you're seeing, hearing, smelling, tasting, and feeling.

You never know what past life you will enter or at what moment in your past lifetime you will arrive. It could be when you were a child, but not always. When I entered my lifetime as George, a man living in a Celtic land in 1643, he was age 40. Whatever your age at the beginning of your past-life memory, the regressionist will ask what you're wearing, what you're seeing in front of you (buildings, terrain, people), plus what your name is, what year it is, and what sex you are. There's usually significance to the day that you arrived, so the regressionist will likely ask why this day is significant. Amazingly, you will know the answers to most, if not all, of these questions.

Once you've learned all that is important about the time and location where you first arrived in the past-life memory, the regressionist will suggest that you move forward to the next significant day in that lifetime, at which point you'll instantly find yourself in new circumstances. Again, the regressionist will ask you what age you are, what you're seeing around you, what you're wearing, and why the day is significant. In most cases, this will be a day where something occurred that had a valuable impact on your soul. Sometimes it's a positive memory, but like most good stories, there might also be conflict.

Eventually, the regressionist will suggest that you move forward in time to the day of your death in this past life. And together, you will learn how you died and why. In my own regression experiences, my regressionist always took me into the spirit world following my passing in that lifetime so that I could get a higher perspective of the significant lessons my spirit and soul gained from that lifetime. And every time I've had a past-life regression, the lessons learned were related to something I was dealing with in my current lifetime. This might not be the case for you, but it has been for me thus far.

My favorite books on past-life regression are written by Dr. Brian Weiss. If interested, I recommend that you check out these three books: (1) *Many Lives, Many Masters*, (2) *Through Time into Healing*, and (3) *Only Love Is Real*.

—⚡—

Can anyone be hypnotized for a past-life regression?

Yes, anyone can be hypnotized for a past-life regression, but some people require a few sessions before they have a rewarding experience. In other words, some people have difficulty relaxing and trusting that everything is going to be okay. Even though hypnosis is completely safe, people have a lot of misconceptions about it and fear what they don't know. Their anxiety can be distracting enough that some people need a few practice sessions. Once they can relax enough to follow the regressionist's suggestions without being nervous, they will have a successful past-life experience.

—⚉—

How does a past-life regression differ from a psychic telling me about my past lives?

This is what I love about this experience. With a past-life regression, you can actually feel the body of the personality you were in the past life as well as that person's emotions. You can see the land around you. You can smell the dirt, grass, or farmland. You can taste the food. And you know what that person was thinking. You aren't smelling with your nose or tasting with your tongue, however; all of these senses are taking place in your mind—just like any other memory.

This is what I call a "personal experience" versus a "vicarious experience." Personal experiences are visceral, a combination of intuitive and physical. I, for instance, could feel the pain of grief in my chest when losing a loved one in a past life.

Vicarious experiences are cerebral (mental). When someone tells you to imagine something, it's strictly an intellectual experience based on information you are given from an outside source.

So when a psychic tells you about your past life, you can only imagine what she is telling you. It's not a memory in the way that you can remember eating breakfast this morning. It's merely information that someone else has told you. If she tells you that you were a priest in Italy, that information might be interesting, but it's not an experience.

Like your recall of breakfast this morning, the past-life regression is also your memory. I've found that as the past-life regression continues, it becomes a multisensory experience, which helps me to recognize that I'm not making it up. The information begins popping into my mind like something I had forgotten but now remember.

Although my regressions usually begin with me just "knowing" the answers to my regressionist's questions (what is known as claircognizance), they progress into an experience of seeing pictures or movies in my mind's eye, smelling what's around me at that moment in time, hearing the sounds, tasting the flavors, and feeling the air, my clothing, and everything I'm touching. I also begin to experience the emotions I was experiencing at that time in that life.

The difference between the personal and vicarious experience is like night and day. In the first (personal experience), you drive a car for the first time. Whether you're good at driving or not, you "know" what that experience is truly like. In the second (vicarious experience), you are told what it's like to drive a car. Because the vicarious experience is cerebral, you might think you'll be good at driving because it sounds easy, but we all know that it's nowhere near the same as actually doing it. Just sit in a car with a teenager who is driving for the first time, and you'll recognize this is true.

—⁓—

How does one know which lifetime we'll revisit during a past-life regression?

We really have little control over what lifetime we'll visit during a past-life regression. The best we can do is set an intention, and sometimes our intention is fulfilled, but only if that's in our best interest.

We can intend to go to our most previous lifetime, which of course means little to our soul since there's no time in the spirit world. But it's certainly possible that we might visit the most recent lifetime in chronological history as we know it.

In my own investigation of the afterlife, including my own past-life regressions, we tend to go to the lifetime that is most significant for what we need to learn at the moment we get the regression. So if you need to recall lessons you learned about self-confidence, you'll probably recall a lifetime that dealt with that issue. If you need to remember lessons you learned about dependency, you'll likely visit a lifetime that had significant experiences around that issue.

I actually recommend that you set the intention to visit a past life that holds significant wisdom around an issue with which you're currently dealing. This way, you'll not only experience a past-life memory, but you'll also recall lessons you learned in a past life that can be beneficial to you now.

—w—

Might one visit the same lifetime in two or three regressions?

Sure, this is quite possible. The reason we might visit the same lifetime in more than one regression is because practitioners typically only give past-life regressions an allotted time. So if we need more than, say, 90 minutes to extract the insight we need from a past life, we just might visit that lifetime again in a future regression.

I personally have never visited the same past life twice. But if you do, it won't be to repeat the memories that you already experienced in the earlier regressions. It will more likely be to recall additional memories from that lifetime that hold valuable lessons for you in this lifetime. So don't ever resist your regression experience. Just trust the Universe to make the choice for you, and then simply let it unfold.

—w—

If we live multiple lifetimes as different people, how will I recognize my loved ones in spirit during a reading or when I die and go to the spirit world myself?

This goes back to the relationship between soul and spirit. Since it is our soul that reincarnates via a new spirit, our spirit will always be available and recognizable in the spirit world. Therefore, when I pass and return to the afterlife, the spirit of Bob Olson will always be available to communicate through mediums or greet my loved ones when they pass and come home to the hereafter. And since our soul has signature characteristics that are identifiable, we are able to recognize those signature characteristics easily.

So every spirit that comes from our soul will also be recognized by other souls. Therefore, if my soul reincarnates as a man in one life, a woman in another, and a dog in another, my wife's soul will always recognize me in all those lifetimes. It's kind of like when children wear Halloween costumes. We can always identify them by their eyes, voices, or mannerisms, even though they are largely disguised by their costume.

—⚬—

How do we choose which personality from our various human lifetimes to be while in the spirit world?

This question is a bit like asking whether we as humans choose to be like we were as a child, as a teenager, as a young adult, or as an older adult. Whether we're referring to our human personality or our soul personality, the answer is that we are a combination of all of them.

Our soul doesn't choose any of the personalities of its many lives. Our soul chooses its own signature personality, which continues to evolve with each new lifetime of experiences. Therefore, just as we can usually recognize an adult whom we haven't seen since they were a child, souls also retain a signature energy about them such that other souls can recognize them even as they evolve.

But that's our soul. How about our spirit? If you've read this book thus far, I suspect you already know that our spirit never really changes its personality. As mentioned earlier in this book in the section on spirits, angels, and ghosts—specifically, under the question "What age are we in the spirit world?"—a spirit might show itself to a medium, for example, as appearing at a younger age than when he passed because he felt the most joyful and vibrant at that age. In this way, we can choose to show ourselves in any way we prefer. But we, as spiritual beings, mainly do this for the benefit of our loved ones on the physical plane. People in spirit naturally want their loved ones to recognize them. In reality, however, spiritual beings relate more to their whole self—their soul—than any individual spirit.

To use another analogy, most people have a slightly different personality at work than they do at home and still another slightly different personality when with their softball team, therapist, or book club. Although not everyone would recognize it in herself, we morph a little depending upon our peer group. In truth, we are none of these individual personalities. We are all of them. And the same is true for our souls in the spiritual realm.

—∿∿—

Who determines what souls become our relatives and friends in each lifetime? Do we have pre-birth agreements with other souls?

Yes, we do have pre-birth agreements with other souls before we are born into this life. And it is our souls that make those choices and agreements. But our souls are not alone in these decisions. Our spirit guides and elders assist us.

The foresight necessary to choose our relationships is probably beyond our human comprehension because the possibilities are infinite. When we choose our parents, for example, we must take into account what each of their souls desire in order to fulfill the experiences they want to have as humans. But since each human being has free will, our souls must take into account the vast possible choices that each person in our life might make and whether one of those potential choices could lead us to have an experience we wish to have.

So for example, if my father came into this life with the potential of taking his own life, my soul would have to agree that this possibility is an experience that would benefit me in some way. This would be true for all my relationships. Does my soul want to have the experience of losing a parent to suicide? How about a sibling, a friend, a coworker, or a relative? Each of these experiences would be a different experience, so they each have to be determined, as would the experience of having a parent, sibling, friend, coworker, or relative who had suicidal impulses but did not take his or her life. That experience holds its own lessons and growth.

When we think of the endless possible experiences that exist, we can appreciate the immense forethought and responsibility that goes into pre-birth planning. Our souls choose people who will enter our lives in various capacities—and at various times—who will help us to have the experiences we want to have during this lifetime. But the benefit must be mutual, meaning that we must also help them to have the experiences they hope to have in this lifetime.

Probably the best books written on this subject are those by Robert Schwartz, which I mentioned earlier. They are titled *Your Soul's Plan* and *Your Soul's Gift*.

—⚹—

If we chart our lives before birth, how much of our lives are set in stone and destined to occur?

What is predestined and set in stone is what exists at the time of birth. So the parents and older siblings as well as any other living relatives are predestined. The physical and mental conditions of the baby are also predestined. So if the baby is born perfectly healthy, that is predestined. If the baby is born with physical or mental conditions that are outside what's considered healthy or normal, that too is predetermined as are the child's hair, skin, and eye colors. Where in the world the baby is born, the socioeconomic conditions, the climate, the culture, the crime rate, etc., are all predetermined. All of this can change once the child is born based on the freewill choices of the people around him, but these immediate conditions are choices the soul made for the spirit's entry into the world.

Once the spirit begins its physical life after birth, everything from this point is a "potential." Since the soul cannot predict how physical beings will act, including the actions and choices of its own spirit now in a physical body, the soul's plans for this human being can only be "influenced" by the soul and spirit guides, but nothing is set in stone.

Potentials include innate characteristics within the DNA of the human being that also influence him. Some human beings have a high IQ; others have a high sexual drive; others are very competitive; others are wired to experience depression, anger, or anxiety; others are drawn toward alcohol; and still others have a flair for sports or flying airplanes or mathematics. Sometimes these innate characteristics are further influenced by the people in the person's life (parents, mentors, friends), yet the predisposed potential already existed.

So for example, there is no predestined plan for someone to die on some particular date. Soul plans are not that specific. Instead, a soul might choose to live a brief life because this experience will give that soul some childhood experiences the soul wishes to know, but it will also give other souls (the souls of the parents, for example) the experience of losing a child.

Okay, so using this example, the child is predestined to pass at a young age, but exactly when and how he dies is determined by the soul and its guides. As the child reaches age four, for instance, the soul and its guides might determine that the souls of everyone who knows the boy would gain the most growth if he passes due to a prolonged illness. Or they might recognize that more people would benefit if his death was sudden and tragic, such as by getting hit by a car.

The boy's soul knows that he will pass around the age of four or five. But depending upon an infinite number of factors—including choices made by everyone who will be affected, world events, historical matters, even political happenings—the exact details of the boy's death are decided in real time. Sometimes an unforeseen opportunity occurs where the soul and spirit guides say, "We didn't foresee that he was going to be on this plane that is about to crash" (it was a last-minute decision by the family for the boy to travel). "But now that he is, it is in the best interest of the people involved if he dies in this accident."

If it was not advantageous to the boy's soul that he pass in the plane accident, divine intervention might prevent him from getting on the plane (for example, he might not make his flight, he might become ill that morning and stay home, or he might even have an intuitive feeling of fear that would stop him from boarding the plane).

So fate determines what is going to happen and approximately when, but the soul (with the help of guides) chooses the details in real time (or at least close to the exact date and time). And it all depends upon the freewill choices of the humans involved and the opportunities that exist. In this way, even if the soul decides at the last minute that the boy shouldn't pass in the plane accident, the boy's life will end in some other way in the near future. If the soul's plan is to die as a young boy, that plan is set in stone. But exactly how and when is the potential.

I do not believe that a soul changes its mind about an early death; that is, I do not believe a soul that plans to live approximately 5 years will later decide to live a full life of 85 years, mainly because all the other souls in the child's life are planning to know the experience of losing a loved one at an early age. I mention this because I often hear people talk about "lost potential" when a person dies at a young age (childhood to early adulthood), but in most of these situations, there never was any plan for the person to live out his or her life. So there's a definite loss of life, but there was never any plan by the child's (or young adult's) soul for a potential future.

—⚬—

What happens to the soul after a miscarriage, stillbirth, or abortion?

Please know that I'm not making any political or religious statements in my answer here. I'm just teaching you what I've learned in my investigation of the afterlife. With that primer, the soul, which is eternal, is not negatively affected by what happens due to a miscarriage, stillbirth, or abortion. At most, the soul has a new experience from which it can learn and evolve.

In both a miscarriage and stillbirth, the soul is in control of this outcome. There's two possible ways that this can happen. Let me explain them one at a time.

Miscarriage or Stillbirth Planned by the Soul ...

One, the mother's soul chose to have this experience, and the baby's soul knew the miscarriage or stillbirth was planned from the beginning.

This could happen as an experience solely for the mother (and, in many cases, the father) that would lead to her (or their) spiritual growth. In this case, the mother's soul would have the experience of losing a child, and the baby's soul would have the experience of living a very brief life due to miscarriage or stillbirth.

This is a very emotional and difficult loss, a physical experience that the mother's soul (and father's soul) chose to know. Even though the miscarriage or stillbirth was planned by the parents' souls, it is of no consequence to their human experience of loss; that is, they will deal with grief the same as anyone else.

The soul of the child, however, knew this was going to be the outcome. So the baby's soul signed up for this lifetime (including this early death) knowing there are lessons that can only be known from this miscarriage or stillbirth experience.

In terms of the baby's spirit (rather than soul), if you understand that the spirit's afterlife experience is an extension of its physical lifetime, you know that the baby's soul learns and grows from this furtherance of its lifetime through its connection with his or her parents—a connection that lasts forever.

Miscarriage or Stillbirth Not Planned by the Soul ...

Two, the second possibility is that a soul had planned to experience life through that child, but for an infinite number of possible reasons, the plan changed, and the miscarriage or stillbirth occurred. There are so many souls involved in a birth and life (mother, father, baby, siblings, etc.) that plans do change at the last moment. In this case, the pre-birth plans of the baby's soul have now been altered, so this soul's experience is different than expected.

In this situation, the baby's soul would be entirely accepting of the outcome. As mentioned, it still has an experience, just not the one originally expected. But the baby's soul knew this was a potential. Souls are used to this in relation to physical experiences. Plus the soul will have many other opportunities to experience another life due to every soul's eternal nature. Possibly, the soul will have another chance at life with those same parents at a future date. Yet the soul is also unattached from this possibility, leaving that choice up to the free will of the mother.

In this possible second scenario, there is also a spirit (rather than a soul) connected with the baby. So even though the spirit's physical experience is very brief (regardless of what stage of the pregnancy the life ended), that spirit will always be connected to that mother (and father) spiritually. Again, as mentioned before, this spirit's afterlife experience is an extension of its life experience.

In the Case of Abortion ...

In the case of abortion, we're now talking about a human being's freewill choice to terminate the pregnancy. Since this is a situation that is beyond the soul's control (because human free will trumps the soul's plan), this situation has some slightly different complexities.

With abortion, if a soul had planned to experience life through that child, the mother's choice for abortion was a known potential. Therefore, the child's soul is neither surprised nor disappointed by the outcome. Just as with miscarriage or stillbirth, because souls are eternal, the child's soul knows it has infinite possibilities to live life through another baby and possibly through a baby from that same mother. The soul intending to experience life through that baby is, therefore, completely accepting of the mother's choice to end the pregnancy. ·

As for the mother's soul, and possibly the father's soul (depending upon the situation), the terminated pregnancy is neither good nor bad. Instead, it is an outcome accepted without prejudice. The abortion is another experience for that soul, possibly an experience that soul has never had before. Since every experience leads to growth and learning, the abortion experience will teach the mother's soul about this unique physical experience, including the mother's experiences around loss, choices, beliefs, and other people's judgments, to name just a few of the questions and concerns that might occupy her mind.

The spirit (rather than the soul) of the child will continue its life experience in the spirit world. Just as I've mentioned twice already, the baby's spirit will always be connected to the mother and father during their lives as well as any other loved ones. So the relationship continues even after the abortion, only now the child is in spirit as the parents continue their physical lives.

I have a true story that might help you to understand the nature of souls and babies. About 10 years ago, I had a loved one who was pregnant for the first time. During her pregnancy, my father in spirit came through while I was talking with a medium on the phone, and my father began describing the personality and physical characteristics of the child. He described the child as a boy who was physically strong and athletic. He said the boy would excel in sports and be exercising all the time because he had so much physical energy to burn.

The reason I'm telling you this story is because the baby who was born was quite different than the one my father described. The child born turned out to be a boy, but he's more of an intellectual. Physically, his demeanor is gentle and calm. And he'd prefer to curl up with a book than play baseball or hockey. But what makes this story interesting is that the boy my father described did arrive about two years later with the same parents. And he was exactly the boy my father illustrated through the medium.

Now I don't claim to know exactly what happened here. But I speculate that the athletic boy's soul and the intellectual boy's soul decided to switch at some point during the pregnancy. There could be a million reasons why, but I can tell you for sure that the order that these boys came into this world has shaped their personalities and demeanors. They wouldn't be who they are today if they showed up in this world in a different order.

One possibility is that the soul of the intellectual boy might not have chosen his parents until after the soul of the athletic boy was already planning to be born. In this case, for some unknown reason, they decided the intellectual boy should arrive in the physical world first. So the soul of the athletic boy agreed to wait two physical years (a mere blink of an eye in the spiritual realm) before beginning his physical life. And the intellectual boy arrived first with the plan for him to be a big brother.

This experience taught me that the souls of babies are not permanently decided until the child is born. In this example, the soul of the athletic boy and the soul of the intellectual boy decided to change the order of their births *during* the pregnancy.

—⁓—

Do we have to reincarnate again, or do we have a choice?

I have answered this earlier in this book, so I'll only touch upon it briefly here in case you don't remember. The answer is that our souls have free will, so our souls always have a choice. But it's likely that our souls will reincarnate again because souls are able to be detached from physical life, which means they are not apt to avoid reincarnating due to fear of another arduous lifetime.

Your personality—your consciousness—associates more with your spirit than your soul. So if you've had a difficult life, the good news is that your spirit will not endure another lifetime. As mentioned many times now in this book, it is our souls that reincarnate, not our spirits. So the nonphysical part of you that you most identify with is your spirit, and your spirit will not experience another life, but your soul most likely will via another spirit.

—◊◊◊—

Is there such a concept as a soul mate?

This is really a matter of perspective. If you think of a soul mate as another soul whom you are meant to live life after life with in a romantic relationship, then my answer is no. We do not tend to have "happily ever after" romantic relationships with the same soul, life after life. Said another way, I don't believe there is one soul with whom we are meant to be romantic with lifetime after lifetime.

But if you think of a soul mate as a human being whose connection with you feels so strong that you must know this person in the spirit world (you recognize your soul-to-soul relationship), then I believe this is possible. However, this doesn't mean that your human relationship is meant to be romantic. I actually believe that some people mistakenly view this soul connection as a sign that they should be romantically involved, but that's often not the case. Just because your souls have a special connection in the spiritual realm doesn't mean you'll have a special connection in the physical realm. Soul mates in this perspective can have relationships that run the gamut from lovers to archenemies.

I think the important distinction to make here is that our soul's relationships with other souls do not translate into the same relationships here in the physical dimension. So a soul mate to me would be the equivalent of a close friend in the spirit world. Still, I don't believe we have just one close friend as souls; I think it's more of a bunch of close friends who make up what's called our soul group. And these are the souls with whom we share many lifetimes, although in varying relationships.

So in one life, these souls might be my mother, my father, my sister, my closest friend, my business partner, my brother-in-law, and my mentor. In another life, these same souls might switch roles to be my classmate, my adopted brother, my neighbor, the policeman who gave me a break when he could have arrested me, a fellow prisoner of war, the first enemy soldier I killed, and the love of my life.

Not everyone in our life is part of our soul group. And some people who play significant roles in our life might belong to another soul group. It's not so much about the significance they play in your life as much as the connection you feel when you're with them—including when you first meet them. Sometimes we feel an instant connection with a person as if we've known them our entire lives. In many cases, this is due to our soul connection. This is my definition of the phrase 'soul mate.'

—⁓—

What is the purpose of past-life regressions?

There's more than one purpose for having a past-life regression.

First, experiencing a past-life regression teaches us that we live multiple lives. Therefore, past-life regressions provide us with a "knowing" that we do not die because our soul is able to experience other lifetimes. In this way, it helps us to recognize that we are eternal. And this knowing has numerous benefits considering that many of our psychological maladies stem around our beliefs, thoughts, and obsessions regarding our mortality, the most prevalent benefit being a deeper sense of inner peace.

Second, past-life regressions help us to understand our subconscious physical, mental, and emotional responses to life's stimuli. Many people suffering with a phobia have discovered that their phobia is related to a past-life trauma. For example, people with a fear of heights learned that they died in a past life after falling off a bridge, cliff, or building. Others found that their fear of lightning stemmed from dying in a past life after being struck by lightning. Many people have healed their debilitating phobias once the past-life memory was brought to their consciousness.

Third, past-life regressions help us to see the bigger spiritual picture around issues with which we struggle in this life. I was once feeling burdened by a sense of responsibility to other people when a past-life regression showed me the lessons I've learned around responsibility in another lifetime. That experience helped me to not make the same mistakes again and instantly gave me peace of mind around that issue. If you finish each past-life regression by moving into the spirit world following your death in that past life, the regressionist can ask what major lessons you gained from that lifetime. These big-picture lessons can substantially advance your spiritual growth.

Fourth, past-life regressions help us to know that we share more than one life with our loved ones. This helps with our fear around losing a loved one and with our grief if we have lost someone. When we are able to know that we will see our loved ones again and will likely share many other lifetimes with them, it can help to reduce some of the anxiety that comes from thinking we will never ever see them again.

Fifth, past-life regressions allow us to see the many roles we have played and the many stages we have played upon, which I believe teaches us to be more tolerant and compassionate toward others. When you realize that you were the abuser in one life and the abused in another, the caretaker in one life and the person being cared for in another, or the slave in one life and the slave owner in another, past-life regressions can be immensely eye-opening. And they teach us some of the most universal spiritual concepts, which include love without prejudice, forgiveness, understanding, and compassion. Furthermore, these experiences help us to view our lives from a place of growth and learning rather than victimhood and misfortune.

—⁓—

What if I experience a traumatic past life during a regression?

Not everyone has a traumatic past-life experience during a regression. And most people who have recalled a traumatic event in a past life, myself included, do not feel as though the regression experience was traumatic. There's a difference between experiencing a traumatic event and associating with that event so that it's traumatic for you. If you're the type of person whose life is filled with drama, then you might be the type who associates with the trauma. But if you are the type of person who does not get caught up in the drama of others, then you're unlikely to get caught up in the trauma of a past-life event.

Any novelist will tell you that there are no good stories without conflict. The same can be said about life. Our most profound spiritual growth comes from the trauma, misery, loss, pain, suffering, and tragedy of our lifetimes. And since we've each likely lived thousands or even millions of lives, chances are we've lived through a lot of trauma.

Consequently, when we experience a past-life regression, we should expect that we might remember a time when we experienced something traumatic. We tend to remember the past-life moments that hold significant insights, so it's quite possible this might include suffering of some sort.

The first secret to dealing with trauma in a past-life regression is to expect it. If you know it's likely to be there, you won't be sideswiped by it. But even more importantly, the second secret to dealing with it is to keep a detached point of view. Don't identify with the person you were in that lifetime. You're not that person anymore. It's not you as a child, and it's not you today. It's not even you as a spirit. It's your soul's experience, and even though you are at one with your soul, it's not you to whom these events happened.

It's important to know (and remember) that your soul is not emotionally attached to what happened in these past lives, so my advice is for you to do the same. When you have the regression experience, you want to view the past life as an observer. In this way, you're watching the lifetime as a movie—from a distance. And you never hop into the screen at the movies to become the main character, so don't do that in your past-life regressions. It really is just a simple change in viewpoint.

In the same way that it can be cathartic to feel emotions while watching an emotional movie, it can be cathartic to do the same during a past-life experience. But when you leave the theater, you don't take that emotion home with you. And I recommend you keep this same healthy distance when having a past-life regression.

So what if you experienced a traumatic past life? If you kept a reasonable detachment during the experience, you simply take home the big-picture lesson or lessons learned from that lifetime. But if you find the regression has a negative effect on you a week or two later, I suggest you work with the regressionist—or a spiritual counselor—to process the experience properly. This takes us to the next question.

—〰—

How can I process my past-life regression if I have questions, confusion, or some type of negative emotional response?

I'm a strong proponent for processing spiritual experiences with a qualified professional. This includes near-death experiences, after-death communications, shared-death experiences, and most experiences you might have with a spiritual practitioner, including mediums, energy healers, and past-life (or life-between-lives) regressionists.

If you've had a past-life regression, you're likely to have all sorts of questions about the experience. And if the past-life moment you visited involved something dramatic or even traumatic, you're going to need to understand how revisiting (remembering) this past-life memory is helpful to you, rather than merely upsetting.

If your past-life regressionist is experienced enough, she should be able to spend time with you (probably for an extra fee) to help you understand what you experienced and how it can be beneficial to you. This is one of the reasons why it can be helpful to be regressed by a hypnotherapist as opposed to a hypnotist. Hypnotherapists are trained in therapy and, therefore, are better qualified to help you process your regression.

If your regressionist isn't qualified to help you process or he doesn't offer processing as a service, you can either find a regressionist who does or go to a spiritual counselor as an alternative. Spiritual counselors might not know a lot about the afterlife or past lives, but they are likely to know that spiritual experiences always hold a valuable message for us. In this way, they can be helpful in taking your experience and flushing out the benefits it holds for you (for example, why you were led to that experience in the first place). From my own experience with past-life regressions, there's always a valuable lesson learned in that past life that is relevant to your life now.

—◆—

How can I prepare for a successful past-life regression?

First, you want to seek out a reputable and credible past-life regressionist. You can do this by asking for referrals from people who have had them and are pleased with their experiences.

Second, it would help if you established a consistent practice of meditation prior to your regression. There's nothing tricky about this. Simply sit quietly for 10 or 20 minutes at a time. I've found that listening to music without lyrics, such as classical music, is helpful. And I prefer to use earphones or headphones to help remove any outside distractions. Then I begin by focusing on my breathing. I inhale to a slow count of four, then exhale to a slow count of four. If you establish a habit of meditating for a few days or weeks prior to your regression, it will help you get into the relaxed state of mind much more quickly at the time of the regression.

Third, show up for the regression in comfortable clothing, don't take anything that might alter your brain function (alcohol, caffeine), and show up to your regression appointment early so you have time to relax after driving. The point here is to remove any distractions that could impede your focus during the regression.

Fourth, keep in mind that hypnosis is entirely safe. You are always in control. You can stop at any time. And the experience that you're about to have is like a daydream, not a sleep dream. In fact, you'll be talking to the regressionist as the regression takes place, answering her questions about what you're seeing, hearing, feeling, smelling, tasting, or knowing. So the key here is to relieve any anxiety you might have about this new experience by reminding yourself that it's going to be interesting, insightful, and completely safe.

Fifth, as I mentioned earlier, set the intention to remain as an observer by staying detached from the past life. By keeping your distance as an observer, you are better able to extract the lessons from the lifetime you recall. The point of the regression is to remember the insights of that lifetime, not relive the drama, chaos, or conflict.

Part Ten

—⚊—

Questions about Near-Death Experiences

What is a near-death experience (NDE)?

As mentioned at the beginning of this book, a near-death experience is when a person dies for a brief time (a few seconds to a few minutes) and then comes back to life. During this brief period of death, from the person's perspective, he leaves his body, views it from above, and then moves toward (and often into) the light of the spirit world. At this point, he is greeted by deceased loved ones or other spiritual beings with whom he will review his life and recognize the lessons from it. Soon, he is told he must go back to his physical life, at which point he finds himself back in his physical body.

In many cases, information that the person obtained while out of their body has been confirmed—for instance, what doctors said or did in the emergency room—that the person lying dead could never have known otherwise.

—⁂—

What are the most common stages one goes through during a near-death experience (NDE)?

These stages differ from one person to another, but there are some common stages that typically occur with most near-death experiences.

In the early stages of the NDE, most near-death experiencers recognize that they are out of their body. In many cases, the person initially sees his body in front of him. If he died during surgery, for instance, he is looking at his body while watching the doctors and nurses attempt to resuscitate him. Many of the people who've experienced NDEs have told me that they were surprised to feel almost no connection with their body. They knew it was their body, but they felt emotionally disconnected from it. Many told me they were surprised at how old and dreadful it appeared to them.

Some people never saw their body but instead found themselves in some other place. Natalie Sudman, author of *Application of Impossible Things*, is a near-death experiencer who found herself on a stagelike platform in front of thousands of nonphysical beings after her vehicle hit a roadside bomb in Iraq. She told me she was riding in the Land Rover one second, then blinked and found herself standing in front of an auditorium filled with these spiritual beings who were all wearing white robes. Natalie became aware that she was downloading information about her physical life experiences to these beings.

Some near-death experiencers found themselves traveling to distant lands. Simply by thinking about a place, they would instantly find themselves there. Some people traveled to see friends or relatives even if they lived across the country or across the world. Others traveled to countries they had never visited before as if they were on vacation, and they were able to describe these locations with detailed accuracy long after their NDE.

Many near-death experiencers found themselves floating in darkness—but not a scary darkness. Many have told me that there is light within this darkness, what some have described to me as a velvety darkness. And many talked about hearing a beautiful melodious sound somewhere in the background of their environment, which they could also smell, feel, and taste (their senses were all connected). A few described this sound to me as resonating like the faint ring after a wind chime has rung.

From this point, the average near-death experiencer found himself moving toward a brilliant, radiant light that is much brighter than our sun, but it doesn't hurt their eyes. This light emanated intense love and made them feel incredibly safe and joyful. Some referred to this light as God, Source, or Creative Intelligence. What I found especially interesting was that some people said the light came to them (it surrounded them like a warm blanket), while others said that they moved toward it. This is often where the tunnel that we've all heard about comes into play. Those who had a tunnel experience say that they traveled through the tunnel toward this light.

Often, once people reached the light (or the light reached them), near-death experiencers were typically met by a spiritual being (a greeter). I've also had some people tell me that the spiritual being met them soon after they were looking at their body, such as while in the surgery room. This spiritual greeter has been described by people as a spirit, an angel, a saint, a light being, or a religious figure (usually associated with the near-death experiencer's religious beliefs). And still, in many cases, the spiritual being was a deceased relative or even a deceased pet.

Some people met more than one spiritual being, such as a few deceased family members. Others said they were met by one spirit but felt the presence of other spirits nearby. In any case, the spiritual being's presence made the person feel comforted, loved, and safe. The closer the being came to them, the more these feelings grew. And if the spirit communicated with the person, it occurred telepathically. In this way, the spiritual being knew everything the person was thinking.

Whenever the spiritual being was a deceased loved one, there were often messages about love, forgiveness, and pride that the spirit felt toward the near-death experiencer. Sometimes this was a joyful re-union, and sometimes the spirit interacted with a more serious tone, especially if the spirit had instructions for the person about how to alter the course of his life.

Numerous near-death experiencers then went through what's known as a life review. This is where they reviewed their choices, words, and actions in life and felt the impact of how their behavior affected others. Some described this as watching a three-dimensional movie on a panoramic screen that spanned between 180 and 360 degrees around them. In most cases, the spiritual beings did not judge the person for how they lived. Instead, any spirits present usually counseled the person to not judge himself for behavior around which he was ashamed or regretful. The purpose of the life review, the spirits pointed out, is to learn and grow from this insight, not feel remorse around it.

The spiritual being or beings sometimes told the person having the near-death experience the reason he needed to go back or, at least, what he still needed to accomplish in his life. This was when he was told that this was not his time to die and that he would have to return to his physical body and life.

Almost all near-death experiencers admitted to not wanting to come back. Some attempted to argue their case for staying in the spirit world. Even those people with families and other loved ones here in the physical dimension—and who had generally happy lives—usually wanted to stay in spirit. Although some feel a sense of guilt around that admission now that they've returned, especially those with young children, the fact that they felt this way teaches us a lot about our true spiritual essence—there is an emotional detachment from the physical world.

This is not to say that our loved ones in spirit do not have love and compassion for us; they most certainly do, and their love has an intensity that is far beyond our human comprehension. But what we learn from near-death experiences in this way is that those in spirit do not worry about us. They know we are all going to be just fine. They know we are eternal beings having a brief human experience and that we too will return home to the spirit world in what feels like a split second to them.

If I could make a faint comparison that might illustrate this situation, it would be like a family taking a vacation together. And when one family member gets homesick and decides to return home earlier than the rest, that family member is happy to be home and knows that the others will be coming home soon.

In the end, near-death experiencers found themselves back in their physical bodies, at which point they often needed to heal from whatever it was that caused them to temporarily die.

These are the typical stages of a near-death experience. Not every near-death experiencer experiences all these stages and not necessarily in the order I presented. And certainly, there are stages that occur with some people that I have not mentioned. But this is what is common and characteristic of the average NDE.

—⁓—

Why do some people have a near-death experience and others do not?

This answer is the same for why some people have *any* spiritual experience and others do not, including dream visitations, deathbed visions, shared-death experiences, out-of-body experiences, or any after-death communication.

We cannot know for sure why any one person has a near-death experience and another one (under the exact same circumstances) does not. For example, two people might have heart surgery and technically die for three minutes before doctors resuscitate them. If one person has a near-death experience and the other does not, the most logical reason for this (from a spiritual point of view) would be that the NDE is an experience the first person's soul wants to have, and it is not one that the second person's soul wants to have. It's really that simple.

We are each experiencing a human lifetime because our souls chose it. But our soul's pre-birth planning of our life has specific intentions as to what our soul wants us to experience. This is why our souls chose the parents we have and all the circumstances that existed when we were born. The time in history, our location in the world, our physical characteristics, even the positions of the stars and planets—all were strategically chosen by our souls so that our lives would be a certain way.

Given that your soul has specific plans for your life, doesn't it make sense that a near-death experience, dream visitation, or any other spiritual experience might not fit into your soul's plans? Obviously, a near-death experience might alter someone's life quite dramatically. So it makes perfect sense why some people have the experience and others do not. It's all about what experiences fit into your soul's plan, which is ultimately *your* plan as you and your soul are one.

—ɱ—

Why do some people claim to have experienced going to hell in their near-death experience?

I wrote about this subject early in this book under the question about hell, but it's worth repeating my answer here (with some additional comments). While 10 percent to 15 percent of adults who have had near-death experiences have suggested they experienced some version of what might be interpreted as hell, the evidence of near-death experiences indicates two important factors: (1) that the details of what we experience in the NDE are interpreted by our own points of reference (what we believe as human beings) and (2) that the initial experiences we have of the afterlife during the NDE are in direct relation to our expectations of it.

So if you remember that we can be, do, and have anything we want in spirit, then you understand how easily we might create a hell-like experience when we cross over to the other side during the NDE, especially if that's what we are expecting. Our beliefs alone might make it so. Still, the hell these people experience is not what most people think of as hell (a place of eternal damnation). Instead, it is a hell-like environment of their own creation, which they can change at any moment simply by changing their thoughts (although most people who have this experience don't know they can do this).

If we've learned anything from near-death experiences, it is that we can create our own reality in the spiritual dimension. One near-death experiencer told me that when she thought of a field, she found herself in a field. When she then changed her thought from a field to a tunnel, she found herself in a tunnel. When she then changed her thought to being in the hospital with her physical body, she found herself walking down a hallway in the hospital. She said everything felt so real to her that she could feel the warmth of the sun in the field, smell the dirt of the dank tunnel, and hear the echo inside the concrete walls of the hospital. But the point is that all she needed to do was change her thought, and it changed her environment.

Consequently, my investigation has led me to conclude that people who experienced hellish near-death experiences did so because they believed in hell and that they would go there when they died. In fact, there are people whose near-death experience began as if they were in hell until they realized that they could change their environment by changing their thoughts (or calling out for help, which is another way of thinking about a new possibility). Then their hell-like environment instantly changed to a heaven-like environment.

This is just one reason why it's important to read books like this one and learn about life after death. Those people who expected they might go to hell didn't realize they would get what they expected, and many didn't know they could change their experience by changing their thoughts.

According to spirits who have communicated through mediums, everyone in the spirit world who does not return to their physical life in an NDE figures this out eventually, if only by accident. At some point, they'll think about being with their loved ones back home or being at their favorite fishing hole, and then—sure enough—they'll find themselves there. But there are people who have had near-death experiences and didn't have the opportunity to get to this point because they were sent back to their physical bodies before they figured it out.

From my perspective, this is why we have people who talk about their hellish NDEs. Their experiences were real. I certainly don't dispute their stories, and most NDE researchers don't either. Perhaps these were the perfect experiences these folks needed to have. Maybe it served as a wake up call for them and altered their lives in some positive way. After all, if someone expects that he is going to hell, there might be some reason behind it.

I certainly wouldn't let this minority of cases make you fearful about dying. If you've read this entire book and have done some investigating of the afterlife on your own, chances are you know a lot more about transitioning to the afterlife than these people did when they had their NDEs. And my hope in writing this book is to help take the fear out of dying because my investigations have led me to believe that it's a million times better than we can even imagine.

If you want to delve more deeply into near-death experiences, including negative NDEs, I highly recommend P. M. H. Atwater's book *Near-Death Experiences: The Rest of the Story*. What I love about this book is that it's her most candid book on the subject, which allowed her to reveal conclusions that she didn't feel comfortable sharing in her other books.

—⚋⚋—

What makes children's near-death experiences especially interesting?

What's most interesting about children's near-death experiences is that children have fewer expectations and less established beliefs around the afterlife, so their reports about their NDEs are not tainted by these expectations and beliefs.

Furthermore, most children are not able to understand death and have never formed an opinion of life after death, so this allows NDE researchers the opportunity to compare children's NDE stories with the often interpretation-blemished stories of adults. And these comparisons allow us to draw conclusions about near-death experiences from these accounts that have not been clouded by opinion.

For example, children are more likely to call a spiritual being a "bright light that talked to me," "an angel," or "a nice woman dressed in white," whereas adults might give their spiritual being an identity, such as "Jesus," "God," or "my spirit guide."

The younger the child, the less beliefs they have, so their descriptions of NDEs are less likely to be interpreted through the eyes of their religious beliefs or what they've been taught. These children just tell us what they saw or experienced rather than their interpretation of what they thought those things were or meant.

Let me give you two examples. Children have called the tunnel (that many near-death experiencers have mentioned) "a noodle" or "a slide," and they described the light of the spirit world as "the sun" or "a light of love." We generally don't get the details from children that we do from adults, so that is often where children's accounts of their NDEs fall short. But we are more likely to get drawings or paintings from children, which can sometimes provide a better perspective than words.

For the most part, there's a sweet authenticity to children's stories about their NDEs, so they describe them with greater innocence and less interpretation. This helps researchers determine the ordinary stages one goes through during a near-death experience without the associations most adults give to these experiences. And in this way, the children's accounts help us to confirm the adults' accounts with increased reliability. But we couldn't have the depth of insight we've gained about NDEs if not for the adult accounts, so we are lucky to have both.

—∞—

Who decides that a near-death experiencer must go back to his or her physical life?

We can only guess who makes the decision that a near-death experiencer must return to his or her physical body and life. Perhaps it's Source or the person's soul or maybe even the person's spirit guides. It could be all three who make this choice.

If I had to speculate based on my own investigation of this subject, I would guess that our souls and spirit guides make this decision together. Yet I write this knowing that our souls and spirit guides are at one with Source, so in this way, Source is part of every decision.

I haven't interviewed a near-death experiencer who knew the identity of the decision maker, although most recall who gave them the news. Some people just heard a voice say, "It's not your time. You must go back." One person I interviewed heard someone say, "What's she doing here?" And before she had an opportunity to argue her case for staying in the spirit world, she found herself back in her body.

Even if one person were to know who made the choice (in their case) that they must return to their body, it doesn't mean the same would be true for everyone else.

Some near-death experiencers are given the choice to go back into their physical body, but not everyone. Obviously, if they are here to tell us about it, they chose to come back. Who knows how many were given the choice and decided to remain in the spirit world? We can't possibly know that statistic. But for those who did make this choice to return to their life, it was usually due to some purpose, especially considering that most people want to stay in the spirit world.

This purpose for returning to their life might have been to finish raising their children, to avoid putting a loved one through the experience of their loss, or to complete something they hadn't yet started but knew (from their spirit-world perspective) that their soul had intended to accomplish later in life. The possibilities are truly endless, but there is typically some purpose behind their decision.

—␣␣—

Do people who have had near-death experiences know everything about the afterlife?

No, people who have had near-death experiences do not know everything about the afterlife. This is not to say that they don't have a better "sense" of what the afterlife is like—they do. And this is not to say that we can't learn a lot about the afterlife via the testimony of near-death experiencers—we can. What I'm saying is that near-death experiences are subjective, so the best way to use NDEs to learn about life after death is by comparing the NDE data from many near-death experiencers (not just one or a few) and then coordinating that data with all the other afterlife evidence that exists, such as mediumship, deathbed visions, shared-death experiences, past-life regressions, life-between-lives regressions, past-life memories, and the other subjects of investigation that I listed at the beginning of this book.

I have had the fortunate opportunity to question many near-death experiencers, and what has always fascinated me is how their experiences differ. Ask 20 people who have had a near-death experience a question about the afterlife, and you could get 20 different answers. So what I learned rather quickly in my investigation is to ask people about their "subjective" experience and not ask them questions that involve their speculation about the afterlife in general. For example, many near-death experiencers have an experience that they describe as going through a tunnel, but many do not. So for any one person to speculate that we all go through a tunnel in our transition to the afterlife would be inaccurate.

As mentioned earlier in this section on NDEs, there are common stages of near-death experiences, but the details that make up those stages, and any new stages or experiences that are outside the norm, can be as varied and unusual as the landscape of an entire country.

In comparison, just because one person knows the experience of visiting New York City does not mean he also knows what it's like to visit the United States. Asking the New York City traveler what the United States is like is the equivalent of asking a near-death experiencer questions about life after death. The near-death experiencer knows what it was like to experience her NDE, but that does not translate into her knowing everything about the afterlife.

While I chose this as an important question to answer, I don't intend to have my answer minimize the importance of NDE testimony.

Although these experiences are subjective, they still provide us with infinitely valuable evidence and information about life after death.

For me, my interviews with near-death experiencers helped fill in the gaps regarding my understanding about the afterlife in a way that no other afterlife evidence could provide. So my point in answering this question is to recommend that you don't get stuck on any one person's testimony as that could be confusing to you. Instead, learn about the experiences of many near-death experiencers, and then compare and contrast that information with evidence you have gathered from other sources and spiritual experiences as I mentioned at the beginning of this answer.

—⟋⟍—

Is a near-death experience a positive life-changing experience?

For most people, it is a positive experience. As I mentioned earlier in this section, a few have had experiences they interpreted as less than positive, but these are definitely the minority. And for some near-death experiencers, the experience has been life changing. Here are some examples:

Anita Moorjani, author of *Dying to Be Me*, learned from her near-death experience that the cancer that led to her experience was caused by her fears. This revelation led her to write her book and begin sharing her message about fear and healing at lectures around the world.

Dr. Eben Alexander, author of *Proof of Heaven*, learned from his near-death experience that true health can only be achieved when we realize that God and the soul are real and that death is not the end of life, but merely a transition.

Dannion Brinkley, author of *Saved by the Light*, was filled with such a profound sense of service and compassion after his near-death experiences (he had more than one) that this led to his work as a hospice volunteer, sitting at the bedside of thousands of dying veterans, many as they took their final breath.

This answer really depends upon your definition of the phrase 'life changing' because not everyone's near-death experience has led to obvious life-changing consequences. I know one man who has had three NDEs and struggles through life due to the same health issues that led to his NDEs. And I know many people whose NDEs were amazing and deeply spiritual, yet their life has changed very little.

With that said, most near-death experiencers—even those whose lives were not dramatically changed by their experience—consider their NDE to be one of the most enlightening, loving, profound, and memorable experiences of their lifetime. Most say that they no longer fear death since the event, which is much more life altering than it might seem. Even more so, many say that they look forward to returning to the spiritual dimension, yet without wanting to rush through life to get there. On the contrary, most near-death experiencers feel a sense of purpose here, even if they don't know exactly what that purpose is. They know they are here for a reason, and their NDE provided them with a sense of peace in this way. In my view, these insights and results *are* life changing, even if the person's day-to-day life doesn't appear any different.

FINAL WORDS

—ɯ—

HOW LEARNING ABOUT THE AFTERLIFE
TEACHES US ABOUT LIFE

So often, I have the heard the comment that I should focus more on life than I do death. What many people don't know is that my investigation of what happens when we die has taught me as much about life as it has the afterlife.

I can honestly say that my experiences researching this field have made me a better human being. I'm more loving and more compassionate, and I feel a greater sense of inner peace and purpose than I ever did when I never gave the afterlife a second thought. And I attribute this transformation to the knowing I gained about life and death from my research.

This knowing did not occur as one event. It came as a process. More importantly, it was a subtle process that enveloped me gradually as a result of my experiences. Said another way, what I learned about life during my investigation of the afterlife was less intellectual and more experiential. Rather than memorize information, I instead became aware of an internal wisdom that I never before knew existed.

I didn't notice it right away. I first recognized this wisdom in my behavior. I was responding to life in a new way. I was making choices differently than I once did. Without planning it or expecting it, my spiritual experiences stemming from my research of life after death had changed me. And before I knew it, I discovered that my work inadvertently had taught me how to live a fuller life with greater love, joy, and inner peace regardless of whatever drama or chaos might be happening around me.

My most significant growth resulted from my understanding of the concepts I stated in the "Big-Picture Section" at the beginning of this book. I'm not sure at what point it happened, but when I came to know that the purpose of life is to have experiences—which can include negative experiences—and I shifted my paradigm of God from entity to energy, I stopped looking at my challenges in life as signs that I was unlucky or was being ignored or punished by God for some reason. Now I saw myself as a spiritual being on a human adventure where *everything* has purpose, even when bad things happen, because every moment is an experience.

I'll never forget one story told by near-death experiencer Natalie Sudman, which is the perfect metaphor for understanding how our souls think about human suffering. Natalie's near-death experience had pretty much ended, and she was waking up after a roadside bomb had exploded under her vehicle in Iraq. She was in a dreamlike state of mind—half in the spirit world and half in the physical world—when she realized that she might be blind in one eye due to her injuries. Because she was still straddling the ethereal veil, Natalie recognized that her soul was quite excited by this possibility of being blind in one eye because her soul had never had that experience before.

Natalie's soul wasn't concerned, fearful, disappointed, or frightened. It was enthusiastic about this possible new experience that it had not yet known in any other lifetime.

Before I began investigating the afterlife, I might have thought that this idea of our souls being excited about an experience that could involve suffering was appalling. Because I believed that life was meant to be only light, laughter, and lollipops, I would not have been able to wrap my mind around this concept that life is about experiences. But now that my research has taught me otherwise, I am free from the suffering that comes from interpreting challenging experiences as punishment, bad luck, or being ignored by God. And while this change in perspective will not eliminate all suffering, it certainly reduces the mental and emotional anguish that comes from these beliefs.

My investigation of life after death has taught me that experience is what happens to us, and it is our free will that gives us the choice of how to respond to what happens to us. Take any experience that most people would consider as negative, and I can find you one person who reacts to that experience as a victim and one person who reacts to that experience by making the best of it. The first person will experience more misery than the second, and all due to a single paradigm shift.

Because of my fascination with death and what follows it, I now understand why Source and our souls allow such tragic events to happen. And I also understand the spiritual depth of these people who keep smiling in spite of their suffering. They inspire us, of course, but even more, they exemplify the power of our spirit. These people respond to life with love, which is all that our souls know in the spirit world. And they remind us through their freewill choices that we can be joyful and loving in the face of challenges too.

I don't know how I would respond to every tragic possibility in life, but I know that my investigation of the afterlife has given me a greater chance for making the best of what happens rather than falling into victimhood. Even in my daily life, I live with less fear and greater inner peace when faced with challenges. My understanding of why bad things are allowed to happen to innocent people—children included—helps me to focus my compassion on their suffering rather than get paralyzed by blame, fear, and judgment. And so I believe that learning about life after death does teach us about life, which is one more reason why I wrote this book.

I hope that you have gained some benefit from my 15 years of investigation and the 3 years it took me to write this book. But I will end my writing the same way that I started it, which is to encourage you to find your own answers about the afterlife. Don't take my word for any of this. Don't take anyone's word for it. Become your own afterlife investigator, gather your own evidence, and then draw your own conclusions. If this book inspires you to do that alone, my efforts in writing it have been successful.

You have my very best wishes for an adventurous journey!

With heartfelt love,

Bob Olson

About the Author

A former skeptic and private investigator, Bob Olson has been an afterlife investigator and psychic medium researcher since 1999.

Bob graduated from college in 1985 with a degree in criminology. In 1997, Bob's father died of lung cancer at the age of 64. The event ignited spiritual questions for Bob that he'd never before considered. Is there life after death? If so, what evidence exists to prove it? And if one could prove the existence of an afterlife, was it also possible to know if our deceased loved ones exist in this afterlife, if they are okay, and if they are watching over us? Bob decided to use his skills as a private investigator to obtain answers, and this was the catalyst for Bob's investigation into the afterlife.

Bob's research of the afterlife led him to create **BestPsychicMediums. com** in 2002, **BestPsychicDirectory.com** in 2007, and **AfterlifeTV. com** in 2011. Afterlife TV is the most recent of Bob's Internet resources to guide and educate the public about life after death using an online video format. He also offers a course for psychics and mediums available at **PsychicMediumWorkshop.com**.

Bob Olson lives with his wife, Melissa, and their dog, Libby, in Kennebunkport, Maine.

Resources—Books & Websites

There are so many books and websites to recommend—new books arriving all the time and websites changing their URLs—that I've decided to post the list on one of my websites so that I can keep it properly updated. To view my most updated list of resources, visit http://www.BestPsychicMediums.com/resources

Made in the USA
San Bernardino, CA
24 January 2015